Cram101 Textbook Outlines to accompany:

Selling: Building Partnerships

Weitz and Castleberry and Tanner, Jr., 4th Edition

An Academic Internet Publishers (AIPI) publication (c) 2007.

Cram101 and Cram101.com are AIPI publications and services. All notes, highlights, reviews, and practice tests are prepared by AIPI for use in AIPI publications, all rights reserved.

You have a discounted membership at www.Cram101.com with this book.

Get all of the practice tests for the chapters of this textbook, and access in-depth reference material for writing essays and papers. Here is an example from a Cram101 Biology text:

When you need problem solving help with math, stats, and other disciplines, www.Cram101.com will walk through the formulas and solutions step by step.

With Cram101.com online, you also have access to extensive reference material.

You will nail those essays and papers. Here is an example from a Cram101 Biology text:

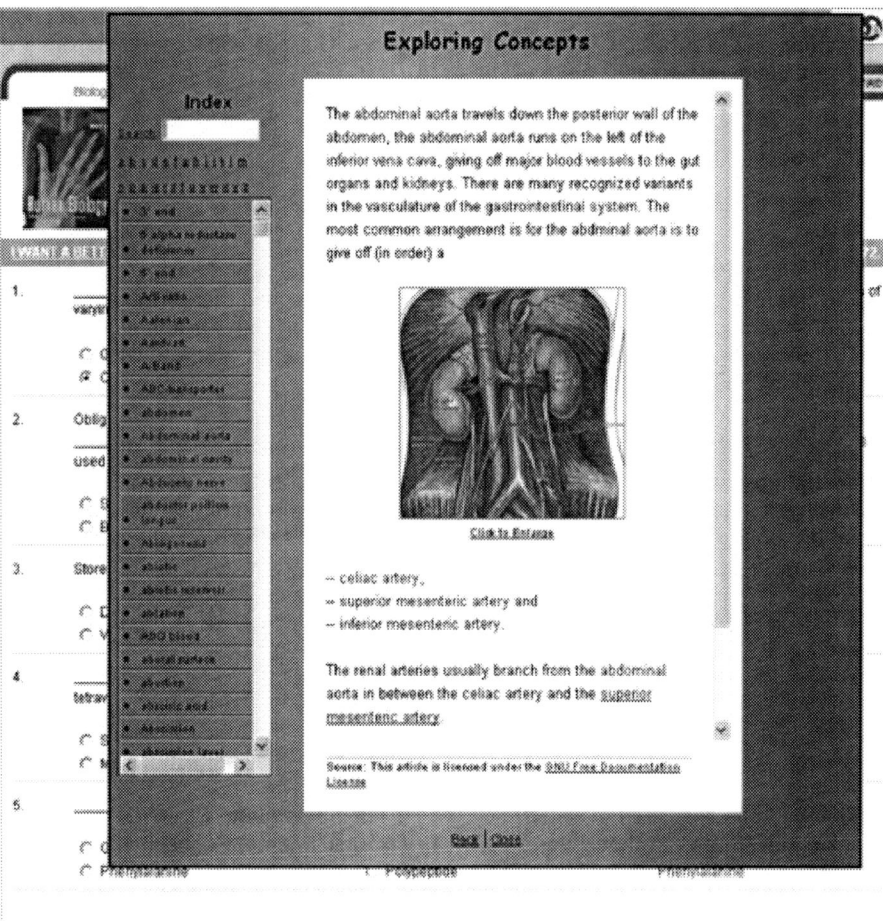

Visit **www.Cram101.com**, click Sign Up at the top of the screen, and enter DK73DW in the promo code box on the registration screen. Access to www.Cram101.com is normally $9.95, but because you have purchased this book, your access fee is only $4.95. Sign up and stop highlighting textbooks forever.

Learning System

Cram101 Textbook Outlines is a learning system. The notes in this book are the highlights of your textbook, you will never have to highlight a book again.

How to use this book. Take this book to class, it is your notebook for the lecture. The notes and highlights on the left hand side of the pages follow the outline and order of the textbook. All you have to do is follow along while your intructor presents the lecture. Circle the items emphasized in class and add other important information on the right side. With Cram101 Textbook Outlines you'll spend less time writing and more time listening. Learning becomes more efficient.

Cram101.com Online

Increase your studying efficiency by using Cram101.com's practice tests and online reference material. It is the perfect complement to Cram101 Textbook Outlines. Use self-teaching matching tests or simulate in-class testing with comprehensive multiple choice tests, or simply use Cram's true and false tests for quick review. Cram101.com even allows you to enter your in-class notes for an integrated studying format combining the textbook notes with your class notes.

Visit **www.Cram101.com**, click Sign Up at the top of the screen, and enter **DK73DW109** in the promo code box on the registration screen. Access to www.Cram101.com is normally $9.95, but because you have purchased this book, your access fee is only $4.95. Sign up and stop highlighting textbooks forever.

Copyright © 2007 by Academic Internet Publishers, Inc. All rights reserved. "Cram101"® and "Never Highlight a Book Again!"® are registered trademarks of Academic Internet Publishers, Inc. The Cram101 Textbook Outline series is printed in the United States. ISBN: 1-4288-0463-3

Selling: Building Partnerships
Weitz and Castleberry and Tanner, Jr., 4th

CONTENTS

1. Selling and Salespeople 2
2. Building Partnering Relationships 10
3. Ethical and Legal Issues in Selling 16
4. Buying Behavior and the Buying Process 24
5. Using Communication Principles to Build Relationships 32
6. Adaptive Selling For Relationship Building 38
7. Prospecting 42
8. Planning the Sales Call 50
9. Making the Sales Call 56
10. Strengthening the Presentation 62
11. Responding to Objections 70
12. Obtaining Commitment 76
13. Building Long-term Partnerships 82
14. Formal Negotiating 92
15. Selling to Resellers 98
16. Managing Your Time and Territory 108
17. Managing Within Your Company 114
18. Managing Your Career 122

Chapter 1. Selling and Salespeople

Personal selling	Personal selling is interpersonal communication, often face to face, between a sales representative and an individual or group, usually with the objective of making a sale.
Communication	Communication refers to the social process in which two or more parties exchange information and share meaning.
Partnership	In the common law, a partnership is a type of business structure in which partners share with each other the profits or losses of the business undertaking in which they have all invested.
Interest	Interest refers to the payment the issuer of the bond makes to the bondholders for use of the borrowed money. It is the return to capital achieved over time or as the result of an event.
Exhibit	Exhibit refers to a copy of a written instrument on which a pleading is founded, annexed to the pleading and by reference made a part of it. Any paper or thing offered in evidence and marked for identification.
Management	Management characterizes the process of leading and directing all or part of an organization, often a business, through the deployment and manipulation of resources. Early twentieth-century management writer Mary Parker Follett defined management as "the art of getting things done through people."
Unions	Employee organizations that have the main goal of representing members in employeemanagement bargaining over job-related issues are called unions.
Union	A union refers to employee organizations that have the main goal of representing members in employeemanagement bargaining over job-related issues.
Promotion	Promotion refers to all the techniques sellers use to motivate people to buy products or services. An attempt by marketers to inform people about products and to persuade them to participate in an exchange.
Competition	In business, competition occurs when rival organizations with similar products and services attempt to gain customers.
Manager	A person who is formally responsible for supporting the work efforts of other people is a manager.
Contribution	In business organization law, the cash or property contributed to a business by its owners is referred to as contribution.
Marketing	The American Marketing Association suggests that Marketing is "the process of planning and executing the pricing, promotion, and distribution of goods, ideas, and services to create exchanges that satisfy individual and organizational goals."
Advertising	Advertising refers to paid, nonpersonal communication through various media by organizations and individuals who are in some way identified in the advertising message.
Mass media	Mass media refers to non-personal channels of communication that allow a message to be sent to many individuals at one time.
Incentive	A reward offered by a marketer to a prospective customer in return for furnishing information or making a purchase is referred to as an incentive.
Publicity	Publicity refers to any information about an individual, product, or organization that's distributed to the public through the media and that's not paid for or controlled by the seller.
Sponsorship	When the advertiser assumes responsibility for the production and usually the content of a television program as well as the advertising that appears within it, we have sponsorship.
Word of mouth	People influencing each other during their face-to-face converzations is called word of mouth.
Buyer	A buyer refers to a role in the buying center with formal authority and responsibility to select the supplier and negotiate the terms of the contract.
Credibility	The extent to which a source is perceived as having knowledge, skill, or experience relevant to a

Chapter 1. Selling and Salespeople

Chapter 1. Selling and Salespeople

	communication topic and can be trusted to give an unbiased opinion or present objective information on the issue is called credibility.
Content	Content refers to all digital information included on a website, including the presentation form-text, video, audio, and graphics.
Trust	Trust refers to a legal relationship in which a person who has legal title to property has the duty to hold it for the use or benefit of another person. The term is also used in a general sense to mean confidence reposed in one person by another.
Trade show	A type of exhibition or forum where manufacturers can display their products to current as well as prospective buyers is referred to as trade show.
Integrated Marketing Communication	Integrated Marketing Communication is a management concept that is designed to make all aspects of marketing communication such as advertising, sales promotion, public relations, and direct marketing work together as a unified force.
Marketing communication	The communication components of marketing, which include public relations, advertising, personal selling, and sales promotion is a marketing communication.
Product	Any physical good, service, or idea that satisfies a want or need is called product. Product in project management is a physical entity created as a result of project work.
Broker	An agent who bargains or carries on negotiations in behalf of the principal as an intermediary between the latter and third persons in transacting business relative to the acquisition of contractual rights, or to the sale or purchase of property the custody of which is not entrusted to him or her for the purpose of discharging the agency is called a broker.
Advertising campaign	A comprehensive advertising plan that consists of a series of messages in a variety of media that center on a single theme or idea is referred to as an advertising campaign.
Learning organization	A firm, which values continuous learning and is consistently looking to adapt and change with its environment is referred to as learning organization.
Organizational learning	Organizational learning is an area of knowledge within organizational theory that studies models and theories about the way an organization learns and adapts.
Distribution	Distribution is one of the four aspects of marketing. A distribution business is the middleman between the manufacturer and retailer or (usually)in commercial or industrial the business customer.
Users	Users refer to people in the organization who actually use the product or service purchased by the buying center.
Channel	Channel, in communications (sometimes called communications channel), refers to the medium used to convey information from a sender (or transmitter) to a receiver.
Cooperative	A business owned and controlled by the people who use it, producers, consumers, or workers with similar needs who pool their resources for mutual gain is called cooperative.
Relationship marketing	Marketing whose goal is to keep individual customers over time by offering them products that exactly meet their requirements is called relationship marketing.
Loyalty	Marketers tend to define customer loyalty as making repeat purchases. Some argue that it should be defined attitudinally as a strongly positive feeling about the brand.
Supply chain management	The integration and organization of information and logistic activities across firms in a supply chain for the purpose of creating and delivering goods and services that provide value to customers is supply chain management.
Supply chain	The sequence of linked activities that must be performed by various organizations to move goods from the sources of raw materials to ultimate consumers is referred to as supply chain.

Go to **Cram101.com** for the Practice Tests for this Chapter.

Chapter 1. Selling and Salespeople

Chapter 1. Selling and Salespeople

Inventory	Inventory refers to physical material purchased from suppliers, which may or may not be reworked for sale to customers. A unique element of services-the need for and cost of having a service provider available.
Holder	A person in possession of a document of title or an instrument payable or indorsed to him, his order, or to bearer is a holder.
Expense	An expense refers to costs involved in operating a business, such as rent, utilities, and salaries.
Capital	Contributions of money and other property to a business made by the owners of the business are capital.
Agency	Agency refers to a legal relationship in which an agent acts under the direction of a principal for the principal's benefit. Also used to refer to government regulatory bodies of all kinds.
Accounting	The recording, classifying, summarizing, and interpreting of financial events and transactions to provide management and other interested parties the information they need to make good decisions is called accounting.
Audit	Audit refers to the verification of a company's books and records pursuant to federal securities laws, state laws, and stock exchange rules that must be performed by an independent CPA.
Warehouse	Warehouse refers to a location, often decentralized, that a firm uses to store, consolidate, age, or mix stock; house product-recall programs; or ease tax burdens.
Principal	In agency law, one under whose direction an agent acts and for whose benefit that agent acts is a principal.
Direct channel	A marketing channel where a producer and ultimate consumer deal directly with each other is a direct channel.
Channel of distribution	A whole set of marketing intermediaries, such as wholesalers and retailers, who join together to transport and store goods in their path from producers to consumers is referred to as channel of distribution.
Insurance	A means for persons and businesses to protect themselves against the risk of loss is insurance.
Customer contact	Customer contact refers to a characteristic of services that notes that customers tend to be more involved in the production of services than they are in manufactured goods.
Stock	In financial terminology, stock is the capital raized by a corporation, through the issuance and sale of shares. A shareholder is any person or organization which owns one or more shares of a corporation's stock. The aggregate value of a corporation's issued shares is its market capitalization.
Purchasing	Purchasing refers to the function in a firm that searches for quality material resources, finds the best suppliers, and negotiates the best price for goods and services.
Tangible	Having a physical existence is referred to as the tangible. Personal property other than real estate, such as cars, boats, stocks, or other assets.
Holding	The holding is a court's determination of a matter of law based on the issue presented in the particular case. In other words: under this law, with these facts, this result.
Estate	An estate is the totality of the legal rights, interests, entitlements and obligations attaching to property. In the context of wills and probate, it refers to the totality of the property which the deceased owned or in which some interest was held.
Mistake	In contract law a mistake is incorrect understanding by one or more parties to a contract and may be used as grounds to invalidate the agreement. Common law has identified three different types of mistake in contract: unilateral mistake, mutual mistake, and common mistake.
Advertisement	Advertisement is the promotion of goods, services, companies and ideas, usually by an identified sponsor. Marketers see advertising as part of an overall promotional strategy.

Go to **Cram101.com** for the Practice Tests for this Chapter.

Chapter 1. Selling and Salespeople

Adaptive selling	Adaptive selling refers to a need-satisfaction sales presentation that involves adjusting the presentation to fit the selling situation.
Emotional intelligence	The ability to understand one's own emotions and the emotions of people with whom one interacts on a daily basis is referred to as the emotional intelligence.
Controlling	A management function that involves determining whether or not an organization is progressing toward its goals and objectives, and taking corrective action if it is not is called controlling.
Empathy	Empathy refers to dimension of service quality-caring individualized attention provided to customers.
Compensation	A payment that is given or recieved as reparation for a service or loss is referred to as compensation.
Standing	Standing refers to the legal requirement that anyone seeking to challenge a particular action in court must demonstrate that such action substantially affects his legitimate interests before he will be entitled to bring suit.

Go to **Cram101.com** for the Practice Tests for this Chapter.

Chapter 2. Building Partnering Relationships

Exhibit	Exhibit refers to a copy of a written instrument on which a pleading is founded, annexed to the pleading and by reference made a part of it. Any paper or thing offered in evidence and marked for identification.
Production	The creation of finished goods and services using the factors of production: land, labor, capital, entrepreneurship, and knowledge.
Outbound	Communications originating inside an organization and destined for customers, prospects, or other people outside the organization are called outbound.
Estate	An estate is the totality of the legal rights, interests, entitlements and obligations attaching to property. In the context of wills and probate, it refers to the totality of the property which the deceased owned or in which some interest was held.
Insurance	A means for persons and businesses to protect themselves against the risk of loss is insurance.
Marketing	The American Marketing Association suggests that Marketing is "the process of planning and executing the pricing, promotion, and distribution of goods, ideas, and services to create exchanges that satisfy individual and organizational goals."
Partnership	In the common law, a partnership is a type of business structure in which partners share with each other the profits or losses of the business undertaking in which they have all invested.
Exchange	The trade of things of value between buyer and seller so that each is better off after the trade is called the exchange.
Product	Any physical good, service, or idea that satisfies a want or need is called product. Product in project management is a physical entity created as a result of project work.
Buyer	A buyer refers to a role in the buying center with formal authority and responsibility to select the supplier and negotiate the terms of the contract.
Interest	Interest refers to the payment the issuer of the bond makes to the bondholders for use of the borrowed money. It is the return to capital achieved over time or as the result of an event.
Corporation	A form of business organization that is owned by owners, called shareholders, who have no inherent right to manage the business, and is managed by a board of directors that is elected by the shareholders is called a corporation.
Trust	Trust refers to a legal relationship in which a person who has legal title to property has the duty to hold it for the use or benefit of another person. The term is also used in a general sense to mean confidence reposed in one person by another.
Cooperative	A business owned and controlled by the people who use it, producers, consumers, or workers with similar needs who pool their resources for mutual gain is called cooperative.
Communication	Communication refers to the social process in which two or more parties exchange information and share meaning.
Leveraged buyout	An attempt by employees, management, or a group of investors to purchase an organization primarily through borrowing is a leveraged buyout.
Buyout	A buyout is an investment transaction by which the entire or a controlling part of the stock of a company is sold. A firm buysout the stake of the company to strengthen its influence on the company's decision making body. A buyout can take the forms of a leveraged buyout or a management buyout.
Vendor	A person who sells property to a vendee is a vendor. The words vendor and vendee are more commonly applied to the seller and purchaser of real estate, and the words seller and buyer are more commonly applied to the seller and purchaser of personal property.

Go to Cram101.com for the Practice Tests for this Chapter.

Chapter 2. Building Partnering Relationships

Chapter 2. Building Partnering Relationships

Trade show	A type of exhibition or forum where manufacturers can display their products to current as well as prospective buyers is referred to as trade show.
Account executive	The individual who serves as the liaison between the advertising agency and the client is the account executive. The account executive is responsible for managing all of the services the agency provides to the client and representing the agency's point of view to the client.
Inventory	Inventory refers to physical material purchased from suppliers, which may or may not be reworked for sale to customers. A unique element of services-the need for and cost of having a service provider available.
Strategic partnership	Strategic partnership refers to an association between two firms by which they agree to work together to achieve a strategic goal. This is often associated with long-term supplier-customer relationships.
Keiretsu	Keiretsu is a set of companies with interlocking business relationships and shareholdings. It is a type of business group.
Distribution	Distribution is one of the four aspects of marketing. A distribution business is the middleman between the manufacturer and retailer or (usually)in commercial or industrial the business customer.
Market opportunities	Market opportunities refer to areas where a company believes there are favorable demand trends, needs, and/or wants that are not being satisfied, and where it can compete effectively.
Purchasing	Purchasing refers to the function in a firm that searches for quality material resources, finds the best suppliers, and negotiates the best price for goods and services.
Compromise	Compromise occurs when the interaction is moderately important to meeting goals and the goals are neither completely compatible nor completely incompatible.
Management	Management characterizes the process of leading and directing all or part of an organization, often a business, through the deployment and manipulation of resources. Early twentieth-century management writer Mary Parker Follett defined management as "the art of getting things done through people."
Comprehensive	A comprehensive refers to a layout accurate in size, color, scheme, and other necessary details to show how a final ad will look. For presentation only, never for reproduction.
Industry	Industry refers to a group of firms offering products that are close substitutes for each other.
Competition	In business, competition occurs when rival organizations with similar products and services attempt to gain customers.
Competency	Competency refers to a person's ability to understand the nature of the transaction and the consequences of entering into it at the time the contract was entered into.
Acceptance	The actual or implied receipt and retention of that which is tendered or offered is the acceptance.
Misuse	A defense that relieves a seller of product liability if the user abnormally misused the product is called misuse. Products must be designed to protect against foreseeable misuse.
Stock	In financial terminology, stock is the capital raized by a corporation, through the issuance and sale of shares. A shareholder is any person or organization which owns one or more shares of a corporation's stock. The aggregate value of a corporation's issued shares is its market capitalization.
Proxy	Proxy refers to a person who is authorized to vote the shares of another person. Also, the

Chapter 2. Building Partnering Relationships

Chapter 2. Building Partnering Relationships

	written authorization empowering a person to vote the shares of another person.
Incentive	A reward offered by a marketer to a prospective customer in return for furnishing information or making a purchase is referred to as an incentive.
Mistake	In contract law a mistake is incorrect understanding by one or more parties to a contract and may be used as grounds to invalidate the agreement. Common law has identified three different types of mistake in contract: unilateral mistake, mutual mistake, and common mistake.
Tangible	Having a physical existence is referred to as the tangible. Personal property other than real estate, such as cars, boats, stocks, or other assets.
Organizational structure	Refers to how a company is put together and reflects some of the underlying ways that people interact with one another in and across jobs or departments is referred to as organizational structure.
Competitive advantage	A business is said to have a competitive advantage when its unique strengths, often based on cost, quality, time, and innovation, offer consumers a greater percieved value and there by differtiating it from its competitors.
Compensation	A payment that is given or recieved as reparation for a service or loss is referred to as compensation.
Authority	Authority in agency law, refers to an agent's ability to affect his principal's legal relations with third parties. Also used to refer to an actor's legal power or ability to do something. In addition, sometimes used to refer to a statute, case, or other legal source that justifies a particular result.
Dissolution	Dissolution is the process of admitting or removing a partner in a partnership.
Marketing communication	The communication components of marketing, which include public relations, advertising, personal selling, and sales promotion is a marketing communication.
Trial	An examination before a competent tribunal, according to the law of the land, of the facts or law put in issue in a cause, for the purpose of determining such issue is a trial. When the court hears and determines any issue of fact or law for the purpose of determining the rights of the parties, it may be considered a trial.
Manager	A person who is formally responsible for supporting the work efforts of other people is a manager.
Economies of scale	A decline in costs with accumulated sales or production is an economies of scale. In advertising, economies of scale often occur in media purchases as the relative costs of advertising time and/or space may decline as the size of the media budget increases.
Commercial bank	A profit-making organization that receives deposits from individuals and corporations in the form of checking and savings accounts and then uses some of these funds to make loans is a commercial bank.
Users	Users refer to people in the organization who actually use the product or service purchased by the buying center.
Logistics	Those activities that focus on getting the right amount of the right products to the right place at the right time at the lowest possible cost is referred to as logistics.

Chapter 3. Ethical and Legal Issues in Selling

Industry	Industry refers to a group of firms offering products that are close substitutes for each other.
Advertising	Advertising refers to paid, nonpersonal communication through various media by organizations and individuals who are in some way identified in the advertising message.
Purchasing	Purchasing refers to the function in a firm that searches for quality material resources, finds the best suppliers, and negotiates the best price for goods and services.
Product	Any physical good, service, or idea that satisfies a want or need is called product. Product in project management is a physical entity created as a result of project work.
Personal selling	Personal selling is interpersonal communication, often face to face, between a sales representative and an individual or group, usually with the objective of making a sale.
Trust	Trust refers to a legal relationship in which a person who has legal title to property has the duty to hold it for the use or benefit of another person. The term is also used in a general sense to mean confidence reposed in one person by another.
Buyer	A buyer refers to a role in the buying center with formal authority and responsibility to select the supplier and negotiate the terms of the contract.
Contract	A contract is a "promise" or an "agreement" that is enforced or recognized by the law. In the civil law, contracts are considered to be part of the general law of obligations. This article describes the law relating to contracts in common law jurisdictions.
Contribution	In business organization law, the cash or property contributed to a business by its owners is referred to as contribution.
Strategic partnership	Strategic partnership refers to an association between two firms by which they agree to work together to achieve a strategic goal. This is often associated with long-term supplier-customer relationships.
Partnership	In the common law, a partnership is a type of business structure in which partners share with each other the profits or losses of the business undertaking in which they have all invested.
Exhibit	Exhibit refers to a copy of a written instrument on which a pleading is founded, annexed to the pleading and by reference made a part of it. Any paper or thing offered in evidence and marked for identification.
Code of ethics	A formal statement of ethical principles and rules of conduct is a code of ethics. Some may have the force of law; these are often promulgated by the (quasi-)governmental agency responsible for licensing a profession. Violations of these codes may be subject to administrative (e.g., loss of license), civil or penal remedies.
Promotion	Promotion refers to all the techniques sellers use to motivate people to buy products or services. An attempt by marketers to inform people about products and to persuade them to participate in an exchange.
Manager	A person who is formally responsible for supporting the work efforts of other people is a manager.
Policy	Similar to a script in that a policy can be a less than completely rational decision-making method. Involves the use of a pre-existing set of decision steps for any problem that presents itself.
Compromise	Compromise occurs when the interaction is moderately important to meeting goals and the goals are neither completely compatible nor completely incompatible.
Deception	According to the Federal Trade Commission, a misrepresentation, omission, or practice that is likely to mislead the consumer acting reasonably in the circumstances to the consumer's

Go to **Cram101.com** for the Practice Tests for this Chapter.

Chapter 3. Ethical and Legal Issues in Selling

Chapter 3. Ethical and Legal Issues in Selling

	detriment is referred to as deception.
Communication	Communication refers to the social process in which two or more parties exchange information and share meaning.
Credibility	The extent to which a source is perceived as having knowledge, skill, or experience relevant to a communication topic and can be trusted to give an unbiased opinion or present objective information on the issue is called credibility.
Vendor	A person who sells property to a vendee is a vendor. The words vendor and vendee are more commonly applied to the seller and purchaser of real estate, and the words seller and buyer are more commonly applied to the seller and purchaser of personal property.
Logo	Logo refers to device or other brand name that cannot be spoken.
Productivity	Productivity refers to the total output of goods and services in a given period of time divided by work hours.
Production	The creation of finished goods and services using the factors of production: land, labor, capital, entrepreneurship, and knowledge.
Exchange	The trade of things of value between buyer and seller so that each is better off after the trade is called the exchange.
Interest	Interest refers to the payment the issuer of the bond makes to the bondholders for use of the borrowed money. It is the return to capital achieved over time or as the result of an event.
Expense	An expense refers to costs involved in operating a business, such as rent, utilities, and salaries.
Compensation	A payment that is given or recieved as reparation for a service or loss is referred to as compensation.
Brief	Brief refers to a statement of a party's case or legal arguments, usually prepared by an attorney. Also used to make legal arguments before appellate courts.
Sexual harassment	Unwelcome sexual advances, requests for sexual favors, and other conduct of a sexual nature is called sexual harassment.
Content	Content refers to all digital information included on a website, including the presentation form-text, video, audio, and graphics.
Complaint	The pleading in a civil case in which the plaintiff states his claim and requests relief is called complaint. In the common law, it is a formal legal document that sets out the basic facts and legal reasons that the filing party (the plaintiffs) believes are sufficient to support a claim against another person, persons, entity or entities (the defendants) that entitles the plaintiff(s) to a remedy (either money damages or injunctive relief).
Discount	A discount is the reduction of the base price of a product.
Competition	In business, competition occurs when rival organizations with similar products and services attempt to gain customers.
Legal system	Legal system refers to system of rules that regulate behavior and the processes by which the laws of a country are enforced and through which redress of grievances is obtained.
Statutory law	State and federal constitutions, legislative enactments, treaties, and ordinances, in other words, written laws are referred to as statutory law.
Uniform Commercial Code	Uniform commercial code refers to a comprehensive commercial law adopted by every state in the United States; it covers sales laws and other commercial laws.
Antitrust laws	Antitrust laws refer to a series of laws enacted to limit anticompetitive behavior in almost

Chapter 3. Ethical and Legal Issues in Selling

	all industries, businesses, and professions operating in the United States.
Agency	Agency refers to a legal relationship in which an agent acts under the direction of a principal for the principal's benefit. Also used to refer to government regulatory bodies of all kinds.
Administration	Administration refers to the management and direction of the affairs of governments and institutions; a collective term for all policymaking officials of a government; the execution and implementation of public policy.
Common law	The legal system that is based on the judgement and decree of courts rather than legislative action is called common law.
Agent	One who acts under the direction of a principal for the principal's benefit in a legal relationship known as agency is called agent.
Authority	Authority in agency law, refers to an agent's ability to affect his principal's legal relations with third parties. Also used to refer to an actor's legal power or ability to do something. In addition, sometimes used to refer to a statute, case, or other legal source that justifies a particular result.
Consideration	Consideration in contract law, a basic requirement for an enforceable agreement under traditional contract principles, defined in this text as legal value, bargained for and given in exchange for an act or promise. In corporation law, cash or property contributed to a corporation in exchange for shares, or a promise to contribute such cash or property.
Acceptance	The actual or implied receipt and retention of that which is tendered or offered is the acceptance.
Damages	The sum of money recoverable by a plaintiff who has received a judgment in a civil case is called damages.
Consignment	Consignment refers to a bailment for sale. The consignee does not undertake the absolute obligation to sell or pay for the goods.
Warranty	A warranty is a promise that something sold is as factually stated or legally implied by the seller. A warranty may be express or implied. A breach of warranty occurs when the promise is broken, i.e., a product is defective or not as should be expected by a reasonable buyer.
Implied warranty	A warranty created by operation of law is called implied warranty.
Reseller	Reseller refers to a wholesaler or retailer that buys physical products and resells them again without any processing.
Misrepresenttion	The assertion of a fact that is not in accord with the truth is misrepresentation. A contract can be rescinded on the ground of misrepresentation when the assertion relates to a material fact or is made fraudulently and the other party actually and justifiably relies on the assertion.
Puffery	Advertising or other sales presentations that praise the item to be sold using subjective opinions, superlatives, or exaggerations, vaguely and generally, stating no specific facts is called puffery.
Inventory	Inventory refers to physical material purchased from suppliers, which may or may not be reworked for sale to customers. A unique element of services-the need for and cost of having a service provider available.
Host country	The country in which the parent-country organization seeks to locate or has already located a facility is a host country.
Marketing	The American Marketing Association suggests that Marketing is "the process of planning and

Chapter 3. Ethical and Legal Issues in Selling

Chapter 3. Ethical and Legal Issues in Selling

	executing the pricing, promotion, and distribution of goods, ideas, and services to create exchanges that satisfy individual and organizational goals."
Specific performance	A contract remedy whereby the defendant is ordered to perform according to the terms of his contract is referred to as specific performance.
Robinson-Patman Act	An act that makes it unlawful to discriminate in prices charged to different purchasers of the same product, where the effect may substantially lessen competition or help to create a monopoly is called Robinson-Patman Act.
Reciprocity	An industrial buying practice in which two organizations agree to purchase each other's products and services is called reciprocity.
Stock	In financial terminology, stock is the capital raized by a corporation, through the issuance and sale of shares. A shareholder is any person or organization which owns one or more shares of a corporation's stock. The aggregate value of a corporation's issued shares is its market capitalization.
Product line	A group of products that are physically similar or are intended for a similar market are called the product line.
Collusion	Concerted action by two or more individuals or business entities in violation of the Sherman Act to engage in a fraudulent practice is referred to as collusion. Collusion most often takes place within the market form of oligopoly, where the decision of a few firms to collude can significantly impact the market as a whole.
Resale price maintenance	Resale price maintenance is the practice whereby a manufacturer requires distributors of their product to sell at certain prices, or set a minimum price.
Push money	Cash payments made directly to the retailers' or wholesalers' sales force to encourage them to promote and sell a manufacturer's product are called push money.
Incentive	A reward offered by a marketer to a prospective customer in return for furnishing information or making a purchase is referred to as an incentive.
Price discrimination	Price discrimination refers to the practice of charging different prices to different buyers for goods of like trade and quality. The Clayton Act as amended by the Robinson-Patman Act prohibits this action.
Tactic	A short-term immediate decision that, in its totality, leads to the achievement of strategic goals is called a tactic.
Commerce	Commerce is the exchange of something of value between two entities. It is the central mechanism from which capitalism is derived.
Allowance	An allowance is an amount of money provided to employees to offset specific expenses such as for travel interstate or to buy protective clothing
Bribery	When one person gives another person money, property, favors, or anything else of value for a favor in return, we have bribery. Often referred to as a payoff or 'kickback.'
Cultural relativism	The suggestion that ethical behavior is determined by its cultural context is a cultural relativism. Cultural relativism involves specific epistemological and methodological claims.
Economy	The income, expenditures, and resources that affect the cost of running a business and household are called an economy.
Boycott	A boycott is to abstain from using, buying, or dealing with someone or some organization as an expression of protest or as a means of coercion.

Go to Cram101.com for the Practice Tests for this Chapter.

Chapter 3. Ethical and Legal Issues in Selling

Chapter 4. Buying Behavior and the Buying Process

Reseller	Reseller refers to a wholesaler or retailer that buys physical products and resells them again without any processing.
Buyer	A buyer refers to a role in the buying center with formal authority and responsibility to select the supplier and negotiate the terms of the contract.
Contract	A contract is a "promise" or an "agreement" that is enforced or recognized by the law. In the civil law, contracts are considered to be part of the general law of obligations. This article describes the law relating to contracts in common law jurisdictions.
Purchasing	Purchasing refers to the function in a firm that searches for quality material resources, finds the best suppliers, and negotiates the best price for goods and services.
Production	The creation of finished goods and services using the factors of production: land, labor, capital, entrepreneurship, and knowledge.
Users	Users refer to people in the organization who actually use the product or service purchased by the buying center.
Capital	Contributions of money and other property to a business made by the owners of the business are capital.
Accounting	The recording, classifying, summarizing, and interpreting of financial events and transactions to provide management and other interested parties the information they need to make good decisions is called accounting.
Advertising	Advertising refers to paid, nonpersonal communication through various media by organizations and individuals who are in some way identified in the advertising message.
Corporation	A form of business organization that is owned by owners, called shareholders, who have no inherent right to manage the business, and is managed by a board of directors that is elected by the shareholders is called a corporation.
Attractiveness	A source characteristic that makes him or her appealing to a message recipient is attractiveness. Source attractiveness can be based on similarity, familiarity, or likeability.
Stock	In financial terminology, stock is the capital raized by a corporation, through the issuance and sale of shares. A shareholder is any person or organization which owns one or more shares of a corporation's stock. The aggregate value of a corporation's issued shares is its market capitalization.
Product	Any physical good, service, or idea that satisfies a want or need is called product. Product in project management is a physical entity created as a result of project work.
Exchange	The trade of things of value between buyer and seller so that each is better off after the trade is called the exchange.
End user	End user refers to the ultimate user of a product or service.
Administration	Administration refers to the management and direction of the affairs of governments and institutions; a collective term for all policymaking officials of a government; the execution and implementation of public policy.
Commerce	Commerce is the exchange of something of value between two entities. It is the central mechanism from which capitalism is derived.
Vendor	A person who sells property to a vendee is a vendor. The words vendor and vendee are more commonly applied to the seller and purchaser of real estate, and the words seller and buyer are more commonly applied to the seller and purchaser of personal property.
Small business	Small business refers to a business that is independently owned and operated, is not dominant

Chapter 4. Buying Behavior and the Buying Process

	in its field of operation, and meets certain standards of size in terms of employees or annual receipts.
Agency	Agency refers to a legal relationship in which an agent acts under the direction of a principal for the principal's benefit. Also used to refer to government regulatory bodies of all kinds.
Insurance	A means for persons and businesses to protect themselves against the risk of loss is insurance.
Estate	An estate is the totality of the legal rights, interests, entitlements and obligations attaching to property. In the context of wills and probate, it refers to the totality of the property which the deceased owned or in which some interest was held.
Ledger	Ledger refers to a specialized accounting book in which information from accounting journals is accumulated into specific categories and posted so that managers can find all the information about one account in the same place.
Authority	Authority in agency law, refers to an agent's ability to affect his principal's legal relations with third parties. Also used to refer to an actor's legal power or ability to do something. In addition, sometimes used to refer to a statute, case, or other legal source that justifies a particular result.
Personnel	A collective term for all of the employees of an organization. Personnel is also commonly used to refer to the personnel management function or the organizational unit responsible for administering personnel programs.
Complexity	The technical sophistication of the product and hence the amount of understanding required to use it is referred to as complexity. It is the opposite of simplicity.
Quality control	The measurement of products and services against set standards is referred to as quality control.
Customer service	The ability of logistics management to satisfy users in terms of time, dependability, communication, and convenience is called the customer service.
Derived demand	Derived demand refers to demand for industrial products and services driven by, or derived from, demand for consumer products and services.
Exhibit	Exhibit refers to a copy of a written instrument on which a pleading is founded, annexed to the pleading and by reference made a part of it. Any paper or thing offered in evidence and marked for identification.
Bar code	Bar code refers to a printed code that makes use of lines of various widths to encode data about products.
Warehouse	Warehouse refers to a location, often decentralized, that a firm uses to store, consolidate, age, or mix stock; house product-recall programs; or ease tax burdens.
Specific performance	A contract remedy whereby the defendant is ordered to perform according to the terms of his contract is referred to as specific performance.
Evaluation	The consumer's appraisal of the product or brand on important attributes is called evaluation.
Assessment	Collecting information and providing feedback to employees about their behavior, communication style, or skills is an assessment.
Competition	In business, competition occurs when rival organizations with similar products and services attempt to gain customers.
Inventory	Inventory refers to physical material purchased from suppliers, which may or may not be

Go to **Cram101.com** for the Practice Tests for this Chapter.

Chapter 4. Buying Behavior and the Buying Process

Chapter 4. Buying Behavior and the Buying Process

	reworked for sale to customers. A unique element of services-the need for and cost of having a service provider available.
Distribution center	Designed to facilitate the timely movement of goods and represent a very important part of a supply chain is a distribution center.
Distribution	Distribution is one of the four aspects of marketing. A distribution business is the middleman between the manufacturer and retailer or (usually)in commercial or industrial the business customer.
Mistake	In contract law a mistake is incorrect understanding by one or more parties to a contract and may be used as grounds to invalidate the agreement. Common law has identified three different types of mistake in contract: unilateral mistake, mutual mistake, and common mistake.
Modified rebuy	A buying situation in which the users, influencers, or deciders in the buying center want to change the product specifications, price, delivery schedule, or supplier is a modified rebuy.
Buying center	The group of people in an organization who participate in the buying process and share common goals, risks, and knowledge important to a purchase decision is referred to as buying center.
Data processing	Data processing refers to a name for business technology in the 1970s; included technology that supported an existing business and was primarily used to improve the flow of financial information.
Marketing	The American Marketing Association suggests that Marketing is "the process of planning and executing the pricing, promotion, and distribution of goods, ideas, and services to create exchanges that satisfy individual and organizational goals."
Delegation	Delegation is the handing of a task over to another person, usually a subordinate. It is the assignment of authority and responsibility to another person to carry out specific activities.
Total cost	The total expense incurred by a firm in producing and marketing a product is the total cost. Total cost is the sum of fixed cost and variable cost. In physical distribution decisions, the sum of all applicable costs for logistical activities.
Total Quality Management	The practice of striving for customer satisfaction by ensuring quality from all departments in an organization is called total quality management.
Quality management	Quality management is a method for ensuring that all the activities necessary to design, develop and implement a product or service are effective and efficient with respect to the system and its performance.
Management	Management characterizes the process of leading and directing all or part of an organization, often a business, through the deployment and manipulation of resources. Early twentieth-century management writer Mary Parker Follett defined management as "the art of getting things done through people."
Value analysis	Value analysis refers to a systematic appraisal of the design, quality, and performance of a product to reduce purchasing costs.
Premium	Premium refers to the fee charged by an insurance company for an insurance policy. The rate of losses must be relatively predictable: In order to set the premium (prices) insurers must be able to estimate them accurately.
Manager	A person who is formally responsible for supporting the work efforts of other people is a manager.
Loyalty	Marketers tend to define customer loyalty as making repeat purchases. Some argue that it should be defined attitudinally as a strongly positive feeling about the brand.

Go to **Cram101.com** for the Practice Tests for this Chapter.

Chapter 4. Buying Behavior and the Buying Process

Trust	Trust refers to a legal relationship in which a person who has legal title to property has the duty to hold it for the use or benefit of another person. The term is also used in a general sense to mean confidence reposed in one person by another.
Trial	An examination before a competent tribunal, according to the law of the land, of the facts or law put in issue in a cause, for the purpose of determining such issue is a trial. When the court hears and determines any issue of fact or law for the purpose of determining the rights of the parties, it may be considered a trial.
Coordination	Coordination refers to the set of mechanisms used in an organization to link the actions of its subunits into a consistent pattern.
Materials management	Materials management refers to the activity that controls the transmission of physical materials through the value chain, from procurement through production and into distribution.
International Business	International business refers to any firm that engages in international trade or investment.
Contribution	In business organization law, the cash or property contributed to a business by its owners is referred to as contribution.
Centralization	A structural policy in which decision-making authority is concentrated at the top of the organizational hierarchy is referred to as centralization.
Logistics	Those activities that focus on getting the right amount of the right products to the right place at the right time at the lowest possible cost is referred to as logistics.
Outsourcing	Outsourcing refers to assigning various functions, such as accounting and legal work, to outside organizations.
Supply chain management	The integration and organization of information and logistic activities across firms in a supply chain for the purpose of creating and delivering goods and services that provide value to customers is supply chain management.
Supply chain	The sequence of linked activities that must be performed by various organizations to move goods from the sources of raw materials to ultimate consumers is referred to as supply chain.
Just-in-time	Just In Time (JIT) is an inventory strategy implemented to improve the return on investment of a business by reducing in-process inventory and its associated costs.
Facilitator	A facilitator is someone who skilfully helps a group of people understand their common objectives and plan to achieve them without personally taking any side of the argument.
Strategic partnership	Strategic partnership refers to an association between two firms by which they agree to work together to achieve a strategic goal. This is often associated with long-term supplier-customer relationships.
Partnership	In the common law, a partnership is a type of business structure in which partners share with each other the profits or losses of the business undertaking in which they have all invested.
Channel	Channel, in communications (sometimes called communications channel), refers to the medium used to convey information from a sender (or transmitter) to a receiver.
Electronic data interchange	Combine proprietary computer and telecommunication technologies to exchange electronic invoices, payments, and information among suppliers, manufacturers, and retailers is referred to as the electronic data interchange.

Go to Cram101.com for the Practice Tests for this Chapter.

Chapter 4. Buying Behavior and the Buying Process

Chapter 5. Using Communication Principles to Build Relationships

Buyer	A buyer refers to a role in the buying center with formal authority and responsibility to select the supplier and negotiate the terms of the contract.
Exhibit	Exhibit refers to a copy of a written instrument on which a pleading is founded, annexed to the pleading and by reference made a part of it. Any paper or thing offered in evidence and marked for identification.
Communication	Communication refers to the social process in which two or more parties exchange information and share meaning.
Receiver	A person that is appointed as a custodian of other people's property by a court of law or a creditor of the owner, pending a lawsuit or reorganization is called a receiver.
Product	Any physical good, service, or idea that satisfies a want or need is called product. Product in project management is a physical entity created as a result of project work.
Closing	The finalization of a real estate sales transaction that passes title to the property from the seller to the buyer is referred to as a closing. Closing is a sales term which refers to the process of making a sale. It refers to reaching the final step, which may be an exchange of money or acquiring a signature.
Nonverbal communication	The many additional ways that communication is accomplished beyond the oral or written word is referred to as nonverbal communication.
Channel	Channel, in communications (sometimes called communications channel), refers to the medium used to convey information from a sender (or transmitter) to a receiver.
Interest	Interest refers to the payment the issuer of the bond makes to the bondholders for use of the borrowed money. It is the return to capital achieved over time or as the result of an event.
Controlling	A management function that involves determining whether or not an organization is progressing toward its goals and objectives, and taking corrective action if it is not is called controlling.
Trust	Trust refers to a legal relationship in which a person who has legal title to property has the duty to hold it for the use or benefit of another person. The term is also used in a general sense to mean confidence reposed in one person by another.
Discount	A discount is the reduction of the base price of a product.
Industry	Industry refers to a group of firms offering products that are close substitutes for each other.
Jargon	Jargon is terminology, much like slang, that relates to a specific activity, profession, or group. It develops as a kind of shorthand, to express ideas that are frequently discussed between members of a group, and can also have the effect of distinguishing those belonging to a group from those who are not.
Transparency	Transparency refers to a concept that describes a company being so open to other companies working with it that the once-solid barriers between them become see-through and electronic information is shared as if the companies were one.
Insurance	A means for persons and businesses to protect themselves against the risk of loss is insurance.
Management	Management characterizes the process of leading and directing all or part of an organization, often a business, through the deployment and manipulation of resources. Early twentieth-century management writer Mary Parker Follett defined management as "the art of getting things done through people."
Assessment	Collecting information and providing feedback to employees about their behavior,

Go to **Cram101.com** for the Practice Tests for this Chapter.

Chapter 5. Using Communication Principles to Build Relationships

Chapter 5. Using Communication Principles to Build Relationships

	communication style, or skills is an assessment.
Content	Content refers to all digital information included on a website, including the presentation form-text, video, audio, and graphics.
Effective communication	When the intended meaning equals the perceived meaning it is called effective communication.
Appeal	Appeal refers to the act of asking an appellate court to overturn a decision after the trial court's final judgment has been entered.
Estate	An estate is the totality of the legal rights, interests, entitlements and obligations attaching to property. In the context of wills and probate, it refers to the totality of the property which the deceased owned or in which some interest was held.
Puffery	Advertising or other sales presentations that praise the item to be sold using subjective opinions, superlatives, or exaggerations, vaguely and generally, stating no specific facts is called puffery.
Production	The creation of finished goods and services using the factors of production: land, labor, capital, entrepreneurship, and knowledge.
Budget	A financial plan that sets forth management's expectations for revenues and, based on those expectations, allocates the use of specific resources throughout the firm is called budget.
Competition	In business, competition occurs when rival organizations with similar products and services attempt to gain customers.
Policy	Similar to a script in that a policy can be a less than completely rational decision-making method. Involves the use of a pre-existing set of decision steps for any problem that presents itself.
Client	The organizations with the products, services, or causes to be marketed and for which advertising agencies and other marketing promotional firms provide services is referred to as a client.
Active listening	Active listening is a way of "listening for meaning" in which the listener checks with the speaker to see that a statement has been correctly heard and understood. The goal of active listening is to improve mutual understanding.
Exchange	The trade of things of value between buyer and seller so that each is better off after the trade is called the exchange.
Consideration	Consideration in contract law, a basic requirement for an enforceable agreement under traditional contract principles, defined in this text as legal value, bargained for and given in exchange for an act or promise. In corporation law, cash or property contributed to a corporation in exchange for shares, or a promise to contribute such cash or property.
Holding	The holding is a court's determination of a matter of law based on the issue presented in the particular case. In other words: under this law, with these facts, this result.
Contract	A contract is a "promise" or an "agreement" that is enforced or recognized by the law. In the civil law, contracts are considered to be part of the general law of obligations. This article describes the law relating to contracts in common law jurisdictions.
Evaluation	The consumer's appraisal of the product or brand on important attributes is called evaluation.
Cooperative	A business owned and controlled by the people who use it, producers, consumers, or workers with similar needs who pool their resources for mutual gain is called cooperative.
Coordination	Coordination refers to the set of mechanisms used in an organization to link the actions of

Chapter 5. Using Communication Principles to Build Relationships

	its subunits into a consistent pattern.
Credibility	The extent to which a source is perceived as having knowledge, skill, or experience relevant to a communication topic and can be trusted to give an unbiased opinion or present objective information on the issue is called credibility.
Standing	Standing refers to the legal requirement that anyone seeking to challenge a particular action in court must demonstrate that such action substantially affects his legitimate interests before he will be entitled to bring suit.
Corporate culture	The whole collection of beliefs, values, and behaviors of a firm that send messages to those within and outside the company about how business is done is the corporate culture.
Authority	Authority in agency law, refers to an agent's ability to affect his principal's legal relations with third parties. Also used to refer to an actor's legal power or ability to do something. In addition, sometimes used to refer to a statute, case, or other legal source that justifies a particular result.
Honor	Payment of a drawer's properly drawn check by the drawee bank is referred to as honor.
Negotiation	Negotiation is the process whereby interested parties resolve disputes, agree upon courses of action, bargain for individual or collective advantage, and/or attempt to craft outcomes which serve their mutual interests.
Economy	The income, expenditures, and resources that affect the cost of running a business and household are called an economy.
Context	The effect of the background under which a message often takes on more and richer meaning is a context. Context is especially important in cross-cultural interactions because some cultures are said to be high context or low context.

Go to **Cram101.com** for the Practice Tests for this Chapter.

Chapter 5. Using Communication Principles to Build Relationships

Chapter 6. Adaptive Selling For Relationship Building

Direct selling	The direct personal presentation, demonstration, and sale of products and services to consumers usually in their homes or at their jobs is referred to as direct selling.
Objection	In the trial of a case the formal remonstrance made by counsel to something that has been said or done, in order to obtain the court's ruling thereon is an objection.
Exhibit	Exhibit refers to a copy of a written instrument on which a pleading is founded, annexed to the pleading and by reference made a part of it. Any paper or thing offered in evidence and marked for identification.
Communication	Communication refers to the social process in which two or more parties exchange information and share meaning.
Adaptive selling	Adaptive selling refers to a need-satisfaction sales presentation that involves adjusting the presentation to fit the selling situation.
Marketing	The American Marketing Association suggests that Marketing is "the process of planning and executing the pricing, promotion, and distribution of goods, ideas, and services to create exchanges that satisfy individual and organizational goals."
Content	Content refers to all digital information included on a website, including the presentation form-text, video, audio, and graphics.
Purchasing	Purchasing refers to the function in a firm that searches for quality material resources, finds the best suppliers, and negotiates the best price for goods and services.
Annual report	Annual report refers to a yearly statement of the financial condition and progress of an organization.
Trust	Trust refers to a legal relationship in which a person who has legal title to property has the duty to hold it for the use or benefit of another person. The term is also used in a general sense to mean confidence reposed in one person by another.
Buyer	A buyer refers to a role in the buying center with formal authority and responsibility to select the supplier and negotiate the terms of the contract.
Vendor	A person who sells property to a vendee is a vendor. The words vendor and vendee are more commonly applied to the seller and purchaser of real estate, and the words seller and buyer are more commonly applied to the seller and purchaser of personal property.
Product	Any physical good, service, or idea that satisfies a want or need is called product. Product in project management is a physical entity created as a result of project work.
Capital	Contributions of money and other property to a business made by the owners of the business are capital.
Advertising	Advertising refers to paid, nonpersonal communication through various media by organizations and individuals who are in some way identified in the advertising message.
Appeal	Appeal refers to the act of asking an appellate court to overturn a decision after the trial court's final judgment has been entered.
Brand	A name, symbol, or design that identifies the goods or services of one seller or group of sellers and distinguishes them from the goods and services of competitors is a brand.
Complexity	The technical sophistication of the product and hence the amount of understanding required to use it is referred to as complexity. It is the opposite of simplicity.
Personal selling	Personal selling is interpersonal communication, often face to face, between a sales representative and an individual or group, usually with the objective of making a sale.
Positioning	The art and science of fitting the product or service to one or more segments of the market

Chapter 6. Adaptive Selling For Relationship Building

Chapter 6. Adaptive Selling For Relationship Building

	in such a way as to set it meaningfully apart from competition is called positioning.
Receiver	A person that is appointed as a custodian of other people's property by a court of law or a creditor of the owner, pending a lawsuit or reorganization is called a receiver.
Buying center	The group of people in an organization who participate in the buying process and share common goals, risks, and knowledge important to a purchase decision is referred to as buying center.
Performance feedback	The process of providing employees with information regarding their performance effectiveness is referred to as performance feedback.
Knowledge base	Knowledge base refers to a database that includes decision rules for use of the data, which may be qualitative as well as quantitative.
Competition	In business, competition occurs when rival organizations with similar products and services attempt to gain customers.
Controlling	A management function that involves determining whether or not an organization is progressing toward its goals and objectives, and taking corrective action if it is not is called controlling.
Bottom line	Bottom line refers to the last line in a profit and loss statement; it refers to net profit.
Authority	Authority in agency law, refers to an agent's ability to affect his principal's legal relations with third parties. Also used to refer to an actor's legal power or ability to do something. In addition, sometimes used to refer to a statute, case, or other legal source that justifies a particular result.
Tangible	Having a physical existence is referred to as the tangible. Personal property other than real estate, such as cars, boats, stocks, or other assets.
Loyalty	Marketers tend to define customer loyalty as making repeat purchases. Some argue that it should be defined attitudinally as a strongly positive feeling about the brand.
Industry	Industry refers to a group of firms offering products that are close substitutes for each other.
Assessment	Collecting information and providing feedback to employees about their behavior, communication style, or skills is an assessment.
Productivity	Productivity refers to the total output of goods and services in a given period of time divided by work hours.
Expert system	Computer systems incorporating the decision rules of people recognized as experts in a certain area are refered to as an expert system.
Evaluation	The consumer's appraisal of the product or brand on important attributes is called evaluation.
Automation	Automation allows machines to do work previously accomplished by people.
Enterprise resource planning	Computer-based production and operations system that links multiple firms into one integrated production unit is enterprise resource planning.
Policy	Similar to a script in that a policy can be a less than completely rational decision-making method. Involves the use of a pre-existing set of decision steps for any problem that presents itself.
Marketing communication	The communication components of marketing, which include public relations, advertising, personal selling, and sales promotion is a marketing communication.

Chapter 7. Prospecting

Product	Any physical good, service, or idea that satisfies a want or need is called product. Product in project management is a physical entity created as a result of project work.
Distribution	Distribution is one of the four aspects of marketing. A distribution business is the middleman between the manufacturer and retailer or (usually)in commercial or industrial the business customer.
Downsizing	The process of eliminating managerial and non-managerial positions are called downsizing.
Buyer	A buyer refers to a role in the buying center with formal authority and responsibility to select the supplier and negotiate the terms of the contract.
Stockbroker	A registered representative who works as a market intermediary to buy and sell securities for clients is a stockbroker.
Estate	An estate is the totality of the legal rights, interests, entitlements and obligations attaching to property. In the context of wills and probate, it refers to the totality of the property which the deceased owned or in which some interest was held.
Mistake	In contract law a mistake is incorrect understanding by one or more parties to a contract and may be used as grounds to invalidate the agreement. Common law has identified three different types of mistake in contract: unilateral mistake, mutual mistake, and common mistake.
Exhibit	Exhibit refers to a copy of a written instrument on which a pleading is founded, annexed to the pleading and by reference made a part of it. Any paper or thing offered in evidence and marked for identification.
Authority	Authority in agency law, refers to an agent's ability to affect his principal's legal relations with third parties. Also used to refer to an actor's legal power or ability to do something. In addition, sometimes used to refer to a statute, case, or other legal source that justifies a particular result.
Tactic	A short-term immediate decision that, in its totality, leads to the achievement of strategic goals is called a tactic.
Qualified prospect	Qualified prospect refers to an individual who wants a product, can afford to buy it, and is the decision maker.
Agent	One who acts under the direction of a principal for the principal's benefit in a legal relationship known as agency is called agent.
Better Business Bureau	An organization established and funded by businesses that operates primarily at the local level to monitor activities of companies and promote fair advertising and selling practices is a better business bureau.
Production	The creation of finished goods and services using the factors of production: land, labor, capital, entrepreneurship, and knowledge.
Purchasing	Purchasing refers to the function in a firm that searches for quality material resources, finds the best suppliers, and negotiates the best price for goods and services.
Vendor	A person who sells property to a vendee is a vendor. The words vendor and vendee are more commonly applied to the seller and purchaser of real estate, and the words seller and buyer are more commonly applied to the seller and purchaser of personal property.
Trust	Trust refers to a legal relationship in which a person who has legal title to property has the duty to hold it for the use or benefit of another person. The term is also used in a general sense to mean confidence reposed in one person by another.
Management	Management characterizes the process of leading and directing all or part of an organization, often a business, through the deployment and manipulation of resources. Early twentieth-

Go to **Cram101.com** for the Practice Tests for this Chapter.

Chapter 7. Prospecting

Chapter 7. Prospecting

century management writer Mary Parker Follett defined management as "the art of getting things done through people."

Interest	Interest refers to the payment the issuer of the bond makes to the bondholders for use of the borrowed money. It is the return to capital achieved over time or as the result of an event.
Contract	A contract is a "promise" or an "agreement" that is enforced or recognized by the law. In the civil law, contracts are considered to be part of the general law of obligations. This article describes the law relating to contracts in common law jurisdictions.
Exchange	The trade of things of value between buyer and seller so that each is better off after the trade is called the exchange.
Industry	Industry refers to a group of firms offering products that are close substitutes for each other.
Client	The organizations with the products, services, or causes to be marketed and for which advertising agencies and other marketing promotional firms provide services is referred to as a client.
Customer retention	Customer retention refers to the percentage of customers who return to a service provider or continue to purchase a manufactured product.
Quality control	The measurement of products and services against set standards is referred to as quality control.
Promotion	Promotion refers to all the techniques sellers use to motivate people to buy products or services. An attempt by marketers to inform people about products and to persuade them to participate in an exchange.
Advertising	Advertising refers to paid, nonpersonal communication through various media by organizations and individuals who are in some way identified in the advertising message.
Publicity	Publicity refers to any information about an individual, product, or organization that's distributed to the public through the media and that's not paid for or controlled by the seller.
Marketing	The American Marketing Association suggests that Marketing is "the process of planning and executing the pricing, promotion, and distribution of goods, ideas, and services to create exchanges that satisfy individual and organizational goals."
Barter	Barter refers to the trading of goods and services for other goods and services directly.
Banner ad	A banner ad is a form of advertising on the World Wide Web. This form of online advertising entails embedding an advertisement into a web page.
Extranet	An extension of the Internet that connects suppliers, customers, and other organizations via secure websites is an extranet.
Media buyers	Media buyers execute and monitor the media schedule developed by media planners.
E-commerce	The sale of goods and services by computer over the Internet is referred to as the e-commerce.
Discount	A discount is the reduction of the base price of a product.
Commerce	Commerce is the exchange of something of value between two entities. It is the central mechanism from which capitalism is derived.
Hearing	A hearing is a proceeding before a court or other decision-making body or officer. A hearing is generally distinguished from a trial in that it is usually shorter and often less formal.
Free trade	Free trade refers to the movement of goods and services among nations without political or

Chapter 7. Prospecting

Chapter 7. Prospecting

	economic obstruction.
Cold canvassing	Generating leads in person or by telephone from a directory is called cold canvassing. A method of prospecting under which a salesperson calls on totally unfamiliar organizations and prospects.
Policy	Similar to a script in that a policy can be a less than completely rational decision-making method. Involves the use of a pre-existing set of decision steps for any problem that presents itself.
Corporation	A form of business organization that is owned by owners, called shareholders, who have no inherent right to manage the business, and is managed by a board of directors that is elected by the shareholders is called a corporation.
Outbound	Communications originating inside an organization and destined for customers, prospects, or other people outside the organization are called outbound.
Inbound telemarketing	The use of toll-free telephone numbers that customers can call to obtain information about products or services and make purchases is called inbound telemarketing.
Customer service	The ability of logistics management to satisfy users in terms of time, dependability, communication, and convenience is called the customer service.
Communication	Communication refers to the social process in which two or more parties exchange information and share meaning.
Warrant	A warrant is a security that entitles the holder to buy or sell a certain additional quantity of an underlying security at an agreed-upon price, at the holder's discretion.
Productivity	Productivity refers to the total output of goods and services in a given period of time divided by work hours.
Privilege	Generally, a legal right to engage in conduct that would otherwise result in legal liability is a privilege. Privileges are commonly classified as absolute or conditional. Occasionally, privilege is also used to denote a legal right to refrain from particular behavior.
Competition	In business, competition occurs when rival organizations with similar products and services attempt to gain customers.
Jargon	Jargon is terminology, much like slang, that relates to a specific activity, profession, or group. It develops as a kind of shorthand, to express ideas that are frequently discussed between members of a group, and can also have the effect of distinguishing those belonging to a group from those who are not.
Small business	Small business refers to a business that is independently owned and operated, is not dominant in its field of operation, and meets certain standards of size in terms of employees or annual receipts.
Credibility	The extent to which a source is perceived as having knowledge, skill, or experience relevant to a communication topic and can be trusted to give an unbiased opinion or present objective information on the issue is called credibility.
Bid	Bid refers to make an offer at an auction or at a judicial sale.
Economic union	Economic union refers to a group of countries committed to removing all barriers to the free flow of goods, services, and factors of production between each other, the adoption of a common currency, the harmonization of tax rates, and the pursuit of a common external trade policy.
Union	A union refers to employee organizations that have the main goal of representing members in employeemanagement bargaining over job-related issues.

Chapter 7. Prospecting

Chapter 7. Prospecting

Demographics	Demographics is a shorthand term for 'population characteristics'. Demographics include race, age, income, mobility (in terms of travel time to work or number of vehicles available), educational attainment, home ownership, employment status, and even location. Demographics are primarily used in economic and marketing research.
Demographic	A demographic is a term used in marketing and broadcasting, to describe a demographic grouping or a market segment.
Preference	The act of a debtor in paying or securing one or more of his creditors in a manner more favorable to them than to other creditors or to the exclusion of such other creditors is a preference. In the absence of statute, a preference is perfectly good, but to be legal it must be bona fide, and not a mere subterfuge of the debtor to secure a future benefit to himself or to prevent the application of his property to his debts.
Complexity	The technical sophistication of the product and hence the amount of understanding required to use it is referred to as complexity. It is the opposite of simplicity.
Outsourcing	Outsourcing refers to assigning various functions, such as accounting and legal work, to outside organizations.
Insurance	A means for persons and businesses to protect themselves against the risk of loss is insurance.
Budget	A financial plan that sets forth management's expectations for revenues and, based on those expectations, allocates the use of specific resources throughout the firm is called budget.
Comprehensive	A comprehensive refers to a layout accurate in size, color, scheme, and other necessary details to show how a final ad will look. For presentation only, never for reproduction.
Revenue	Revenue refers to the total amount of money a business earns in a given period by selling goods and services. The value of what is received for goods sold, services rendered.
Learning organization	A firm, which values continuous learning and is consistently looking to adapt and change with its environment is referred to as learning organization.

Chapter 7. Prospecting

Chapter 8. Planning the Sales Call

Interest	Interest refers to the payment the issuer of the bond makes to the bondholders for use of the borrowed money. It is the return to capital achieved over time or as the result of an event.
Strike	A strike is a nonviolent work stoppage for the purpose of obtaining better terms and conditions of employment under a collective bargaining agreement.
Management	Management characterizes the process of leading and directing all or part of an organization, often a business, through the deployment and manipulation of resources. Early twentieth-century management writer Mary Parker Follett defined management as "the art of getting things done through people."
Warrant	A warrant is a security that entitles the holder to buy or sell a certain additional quantity of an underlying security at an agreed-upon price, at the holder's discretion.
Exhibit	Exhibit refers to a copy of a written instrument on which a pleading is founded, annexed to the pleading and by reference made a part of it. Any paper or thing offered in evidence and marked for identification.
Product	Any physical good, service, or idea that satisfies a want or need is called product. Product in project management is a physical entity created as a result of project work.
Reference group	A group whose perspectives, values, or behavior is used by an individual as the basis for his or her judgments, opinions, and actions is referred to as reference group.
Evaluation	The consumer's appraisal of the product or brand on important attributes is called evaluation.
Modified rebuy	A buying situation in which the users, influencers, or deciders in the buying center want to change the product specifications, price, delivery schedule, or supplier is a modified rebuy.
Product class	Product class refers to the entire product category or industry. All products within a product class shall have an essentially similar pressure decay curve, and operate within a given set of operating conditions.
Demographics	Demographics is a shorthand term for 'population characteristics'. Demographics include race, age, income, mobility (in terms of travel time to work or number of vehicles available), educational attainment, home ownership, employment status, and even location. Demographics are primarily used in economic and marketing research.
Demographic	A demographic is a term used in marketing and broadcasting, to describe a demographic grouping or a market segment.
Retailing	All activities involved in selling, renting, and providing goods and services to ultimate consumers for personal, family, or household use is referred to as retailing.
Organizational structure	Refers to how a company is put together and reflects some of the underlying ways that people interact with one another in and across jobs or departments is referred to as organizational structure.
Gatekeeper	Gatekeeper refers to an individual who has a strategic position in the network that allows him or her to control information moving in either direction through a channel.
Purchasing	Purchasing refers to the function in a firm that searches for quality material resources, finds the best suppliers, and negotiates the best price for goods and services.
Intranet	Intranet refers to a companywide network, closed to public access, that uses Internet-type technology. A set of communications links within one company that travel over the Internet but are closed to public access.
Marketing	The American Marketing Association suggests that Marketing is "the process of planning and executing the pricing, promotion, and distribution of goods, ideas, and services to create

Chapter 8. Planning the Sales Call

Chapter 8. Planning the Sales Call

	exchanges that satisfy individual and organizational goals."
Productivity	Productivity refers to the total output of goods and services in a given period of time divided by work hours.
Consultative selling	Consultative selling focuses on problem definition, where the salesperson serves as an expert on problem recognition and resolution.
Brief	Brief refers to a statement of a party's case or legal arguments, usually prepared by an attorney. Also used to make legal arguments before appellate courts.
Stock	In financial terminology, stock is the capital raized by a corporation, through the issuance and sale of shares. A shareholder is any person or organization which owns one or more shares of a corporation's stock. The aggregate value of a corporation's issued shares is its market capitalization.
Industry	Industry refers to a group of firms offering products that are close substitutes for each other.
Brand	A name, symbol, or design that identifies the goods or services of one seller or group of sellers and distinguishes them from the goods and services of competitors is a brand.
Distribution	Distribution is one of the four aspects of marketing. A distribution business is the middleman between the manufacturer and retailer or (usually)in commercial or industrial the business customer.
Manager	A person who is formally responsible for supporting the work efforts of other people is a manager.
Competition	In business, competition occurs when rival organizations with similar products and services attempt to gain customers.
Trade show	A type of exhibition or forum where manufacturers can display their products to current as well as prospective buyers is referred to as trade show.
Corporate culture	The whole collection of beliefs, values, and behaviors of a firm that send messages to those within and outside the company about how business is done is the corporate culture.
Bureaucracy	Bureaucracy refers to an organization with many layers of managers who set rules and regulations and oversee all decisions.
Consideration	Consideration in contract law, a basic requirement for an enforceable agreement under traditional contract principles, defined in this text as legal value, bargained for and given in exchange for an act or promise. In corporation law, cash or property contributed to a corporation in exchange for shares, or a promise to contribute such cash or property.
Coupon	In finance, a coupon is "attached" to bonds, either physically (as with old bonds) or electronically. Each coupon represents a predetermined payment promized to the bond-holder in return for his or her loan of money to the bond-issuer. The bond-holder is typically not the original lender, but receives this payment for effectively lending the money. The coupon rate (the amount promized per dollar of the face value of the bond) helps determine the interest rate or yield on the bond.
Buying center	The group of people in an organization who participate in the buying process and share common goals, risks, and knowledge important to a purchase decision is referred to as buying center.
Comprehensive	A comprehensive refers to a layout accurate in size, color, scheme, and other necessary details to show how a final ad will look. For presentation only, never for reproduction.
Shareholder	Shareholder refers to an owner of a corporation, who has no inherent right to manage the corporation but has liability limited to his capital contribution.

Go to **Cram101.com** for the Practice Tests for this Chapter.

Chapter 8. Planning the Sales Call

Chapter 8. Planning the Sales Call

Mission statement	Mission statement refers to an outline of the fundamental purposes of an organization.
Trial	An examination before a competent tribunal, according to the law of the land, of the facts or law put in issue in a cause, for the purpose of determining such issue is a trial. When the court hears and determines any issue of fact or law for the purpose of determining the rights of the parties, it may be considered a trial.
Marketing management	Marketing management refers to the process of planning and executing the conception, pricing, promotion, and distribution of ideas, goods, and services to create mutually beneficial exchanges.
Authority	Authority in agency law, refers to an agent's ability to affect his principal's legal relations with third parties. Also used to refer to an actor's legal power or ability to do something. In addition, sometimes used to refer to a statute, case, or other legal source that justifies a particular result.
Client	The organizations with the products, services, or causes to be marketed and for which advertising agencies and other marketing promotional firms provide services is referred to as a client.
Channel	Channel, in communications (sometimes called communications channel), refers to the medium used to convey information from a sender (or transmitter) to a receiver.
Line organization	An organization that has direct two-way lines of responsibility, authority, and communication running from the top to the bottom of the organization, with all people reporting to only one supervisor is referred to as line organization.
Tactic	A short-term immediate decision that, in its totality, leads to the achievement of strategic goals is called a tactic.
Clutter	The nonprogram material that appears in a broadcast environment, including commercials, promotional messages for shows, public service announcements, and the like is called clutter.
Active listening	Active listening is a way of "listening for meaning" in which the listener checks with the speaker to see that a statement has been correctly heard and understood. The goal of active listening is to improve mutual understanding.
Communication	Communication refers to the social process in which two or more parties exchange information and share meaning.
Objection	In the trial of a case the formal remonstrance made by counsel to something that has been said or done, in order to obtain the court's ruling thereon is an objection.
Credibility	The extent to which a source is perceived as having knowledge, skill, or experience relevant to a communication topic and can be trusted to give an unbiased opinion or present objective information on the issue is called credibility.

Chapter 9. Making the Sales Call

Interest	Interest refers to the payment the issuer of the bond makes to the bondholders for use of the borrowed money. It is the return to capital achieved over time or as the result of an event.
Impression management	A direct and intentional effort by someone to enhance his or her own image in the eyes of others is called impression management.
Management	Management characterizes the process of leading and directing all or part of an organization, often a business, through the deployment and manipulation of resources. Early twentieth-century management writer Mary Parker Follett defined management as "the art of getting things done through people."
Product	Any physical good, service, or idea that satisfies a want or need is called product. Product in project management is a physical entity created as a result of project work.
Manager	A person who is formally responsible for supporting the work efforts of other people is a manager.
Bond	A long-term debt security that is secured by collateral is called a bond.
Attractiveness	A source characteristic that makes him or her appealing to a message recipient is attractiveness. Source attractiveness can be based on similarity, familiarity, or likeability.
Buyer	A buyer refers to a role in the buying center with formal authority and responsibility to select the supplier and negotiate the terms of the contract.
Context	The effect of the background under which a message often takes on more and richer meaning is a context. Context is especially important in cross-cultural interactions because some cultures are said to be high context or low context.
Holding	The holding is a court's determination of a matter of law based on the issue presented in the particular case. In other words: under this law, with these facts, this result.
Warehouse	Warehouse refers to a location, often decentralized, that a firm uses to store, consolidate, age, or mix stock; house product-recall programs; or ease tax burdens.
Advertising	Advertising refers to paid, nonpersonal communication through various media by organizations and individuals who are in some way identified in the advertising message.
Composition	An out-of-court settlement in which creditors agree to accept a fractional settlement on their original claim is referred to as composition.
Halo effect	Halo effect refers to a more specific perceptual bias that affects perceptions of others; in particular, the use of one piece of information observed about a person to infer other characteristics that may or may not true.
Compromise	Compromise occurs when the interaction is moderately important to meeting goals and the goals are neither completely compatible nor completely incompatible.
Control system	A control system is a device or set of devices that manage the behavior of other devices. Some devices or systems are not controllable.A control system is an interconnection of components connected or related in such a manner as to command, direct, or regulate itself or another system.
Marketing	The American Marketing Association suggests that Marketing is "the process of planning and executing the pricing, promotion, and distribution of goods, ideas, and services to create exchanges that satisfy individual and organizational goals."
Productivity	Productivity refers to the total output of goods and services in a given period of time divided by work hours.
Production	The creation of finished goods and services using the factors of production: land, labor,

Go to Cram101.com for the Practice Tests for this Chapter.

Chapter 9. Making the Sales Call

	capital, entrepreneurship, and knowledge.
Industry	Industry refers to a group of firms offering products that are close substitutes for each other.
Communication	Communication refers to the social process in which two or more parties exchange information and share meaning.
Trust	Trust refers to a legal relationship in which a person who has legal title to property has the duty to hold it for the use or benefit of another person. The term is also used in a general sense to mean confidence reposed in one person by another.
Economy	The income, expenditures, and resources that affect the cost of running a business and household are called an economy.
Contract	A contract is a "promise" or an "agreement" that is enforced or recognized by the law. In the civil law, contracts are considered to be part of the general law of obligations. This article describes the law relating to contracts in common law jurisdictions.
Mistake	In contract law a mistake is incorrect understanding by one or more parties to a contract and may be used as grounds to invalidate the agreement. Common law has identified three different types of mistake in contract: unilateral mistake, mutual mistake, and common mistake.
Objection	In the trial of a case the formal remonstrance made by counsel to something that has been said or done, in order to obtain the court's ruling thereon is an objection.
Closing techniques	Ways of concluding a sale, including getting a series of small commitments and then asking for the order are called closing techniques.
Closing	The finalization of a real estate sales transaction that passes title to the property from the seller to the buyer is referred to as a closing. Closing is a sales term which refers to the process of making a sale. It refers to reaching the final step, which may be an exchange of money or acquiring a signature.
Exhibit	Exhibit refers to a copy of a written instrument on which a pleading is founded, annexed to the pleading and by reference made a part of it. Any paper or thing offered in evidence and marked for identification.
Channel	Channel, in communications (sometimes called communications channel), refers to the medium used to convey information from a sender (or transmitter) to a receiver.
Warranty	A warranty is a promise that something sold is as factually stated or legally implied by the seller. A warranty may be express or implied. A breach of warranty occurs when the promise is broken, i.e., a product is defective or not as should be expected by a reasonable buyer.
Purchasing	Purchasing refers to the function in a firm that searches for quality material resources, finds the best suppliers, and negotiates the best price for goods and services.
Value-added	A customer-based perspective on quality that is used by services, manufacturing, and public sector organizations is value-added. The concept of value-added involves a subjective assessment of the efficacy of every step in the process for the customer.
Lease	A contract for the possession and use of land or other property, including goods, on one side, and a recompense of rent or other income on the other is the lease.
Advertising campaign	A comprehensive advertising plan that consists of a series of messages in a variety of media that center on a single theme or idea is referred to as an advertising campaign.
Inventory	Inventory refers to physical material purchased from suppliers, which may or may not be reworked for sale to customers. A unique element of services-the need for and cost of having a service provider available.

Go to **Cram101.com** for the Practice Tests for this Chapter.

Chapter 9. Making the Sales Call

Configuration	An organization's shape, which reflects the division of labor and the means of coordinating the divided tasks is configuration.
Promotion	Promotion refers to all the techniques sellers use to motivate people to buy products or services. An attempt by marketers to inform people about products and to persuade them to participate in an exchange.
Options	Options give the owner the right but not the obligation to buy or sell an underlying security at a set price for a given time period.
Consideration	Consideration in contract law, a basic requirement for an enforceable agreement under traditional contract principles, defined in this text as legal value, bargained for and given in exchange for an act or promise. In corporation law, cash or property contributed to a corporation in exchange for shares, or a promise to contribute such cash or property.
Reseller	Reseller refers to a wholesaler or retailer that buys physical products and resells them again without any processing.
Nonverbal communication	The many additional ways that communication is accomplished beyond the oral or written word is referred to as nonverbal communication.
Trial	An examination before a competent tribunal, according to the law of the land, of the facts or law put in issue in a cause, for the purpose of determining such issue is a trial. When the court hears and determines any issue of fact or law for the purpose of determining the rights of the parties, it may be considered a trial.
Credibility	The extent to which a source is perceived as having knowledge, skill, or experience relevant to a communication topic and can be trusted to give an unbiased opinion or present objective information on the issue is called credibility.
Assault	An intentional tort that prohibits any attempt or offer to cause harmful or offensive contact with another if it results in a well-grounded apprehension of imminent battery in the mind of the threatened person is called assault.
Subculture	A subgroups within the larger, or national, culture with unique values, ideas, and attitudes is a subculture.
Authority	Authority in agency law, refers to an agent's ability to affect his principal's legal relations with third parties. Also used to refer to an actor's legal power or ability to do something. In addition, sometimes used to refer to a statute, case, or other legal source that justifies a particular result.
Negotiation	Negotiation is the process whereby interested parties resolve disputes, agree upon courses of action, bargain for individual or collective advantage, and/or attempt to craft outcomes which serve their mutual interests.
Coordination	Coordination refers to the set of mechanisms used in an organization to link the actions of its subunits into a consistent pattern.
Teamwork	That which occurs when group members work together in ways that utilize their skills well to accomplish a purpose is called teamwork.
Standing	Standing refers to the legal requirement that anyone seeking to challenge a particular action in court must demonstrate that such action substantially affects his legitimate interests before he will be entitled to bring suit.

Go to **Cram101.com** for the Practice Tests for this Chapter.

Chapter 9. Making the Sales Call

Chapter 10. Strengthening the Presentation

Communication	Communication refers to the social process in which two or more parties exchange information and share meaning.
Buyer	A buyer refers to a role in the buying center with formal authority and responsibility to select the supplier and negotiate the terms of the contract.
Hearing	A hearing is a proceeding before a court or other decision-making body or officer. A hearing is generally distinguished from a trial in that it is usually shorter and often less formal.
Forming	The first stage of team development, where the team is formed and the objectives for the team are set is referred to as forming.
Product	Any physical good, service, or idea that satisfies a want or need is called product. Product in project management is a physical entity created as a result of project work.
Channel	Channel, in communications (sometimes called communications channel), refers to the medium used to convey information from a sender (or transmitter) to a receiver.
Appeal	Appeal refers to the act of asking an appellate court to overturn a decision after the trial court's final judgment has been entered.
Merchant	Under the Uniform Commercial Code, one who regularly deals in goods of the kind sold in the contract at issue, or holds himself out as having special knowledge or skill relevant to such goods, or who makes the sale through an agent who regularly deals in such goods or claims such knowledge or skill is referred to as merchant.
Trust	Trust refers to a legal relationship in which a person who has legal title to property has the duty to hold it for the use or benefit of another person. The term is also used in a general sense to mean confidence reposed in one person by another.
Modified rebuy	A buying situation in which the users, influencers, or deciders in the buying center want to change the product specifications, price, delivery schedule, or supplier is a modified rebuy.
Standing	Standing refers to the legal requirement that anyone seeking to challenge a particular action in court must demonstrate that such action substantially affects his legitimate interests before he will be entitled to bring suit.
Marketing	The American Marketing Association suggests that Marketing is "the process of planning and executing the pricing, promotion, and distribution of goods, ideas, and services to create exchanges that satisfy individual and organizational goals."
Configuration	An organization's shape, which reflects the division of labor and the means of coordinating the divided tasks is configuration.
Mistake	In contract law a mistake is incorrect understanding by one or more parties to a contract and may be used as grounds to invalidate the agreement. Common law has identified three different types of mistake in contract: unilateral mistake, mutual mistake, and common mistake.
Content	Content refers to all digital information included on a website, including the presentation form-text, video, audio, and graphics.
Advertising	Advertising refers to paid, nonpersonal communication through various media by organizations and individuals who are in some way identified in the advertising message.
Personalization	The consumer-initiated practice of generating content on a marketer's website that is custom tailored to an individual's specific needs and preferences is called personalization.
Purchasing	Purchasing refers to the function in a firm that searches for quality material resources, finds the best suppliers, and negotiates the best price for goods and services.
Interest	Interest refers to the payment the issuer of the bond makes to the bondholders for use of the borrowed money. It is the return to capital achieved over time or as the result of an event.

Go to **Cram101.com** for the Practice Tests for this Chapter.

Chapter 10. Strengthening the Presentation

Promotion	Promotion refers to all the techniques sellers use to motivate people to buy products or services. An attempt by marketers to inform people about products and to persuade them to participate in an exchange.
Pledge	In law a pledge (also pawn) is a bailment of personal property as a security for some debt or engagement.
Exhibit	Exhibit refers to a copy of a written instrument on which a pleading is founded, annexed to the pleading and by reference made a part of it. Any paper or thing offered in evidence and marked for identification.
Users	Users refer to people in the organization who actually use the product or service purchased by the buying center.
Attest	To bear witness to is called attest.
Testimonial	Testimonial refers to a statement by a public figure professing the merits of some product or service.
Testimony	In some contexts, the word bears the same import as the word evidence, but in most connections it has a much narrower meaning. Testimony are the words heard from the witness in court, and evidence is what the jury considers it worth.
Closing	The finalization of a real estate sales transaction that passes title to the property from the seller to the buyer is referred to as a closing. Closing is a sales term which refers to the process of making a sale. It refers to reaching the final step, which may be an exchange of money or acquiring a signature.
Discount	A discount is the reduction of the base price of a product.
Credibility	The extent to which a source is perceived as having knowledge, skill, or experience relevant to a communication topic and can be trusted to give an unbiased opinion or present objective information on the issue is called credibility.
Binder	Binder, also called a binding slip, refers to a brief memorandum or agreement issued by an insurer as a temporary policy for the convenience of all the parties, constituting a present insurance in the amount specified, to continue in force until the execution of a formal policy.
Bleed	Printed matter that runs over the edges of an outdoor board or of a page, leaving no margin is called a bleed.
Financial statement	Financial statement refers to a summary of all the transactions that have occurred over a particular period.
Clutter	The nonprogram material that appears in a broadcast environment, including commercials, promotional messages for shows, public service announcements, and the like is called clutter.
Production	The creation of finished goods and services using the factors of production: land, labor, capital, entrepreneurship, and knowledge.
Vendor	A person who sells property to a vendee is a vendor. The words vendor and vendee are more commonly applied to the seller and purchaser of real estate, and the words seller and buyer are more commonly applied to the seller and purchaser of personal property.
Objection	In the trial of a case the formal remonstrance made by counsel to something that has been said or done, in order to obtain the court's ruling thereon is an objection.
Transparency	Transparency refers to a concept that describes a company being so open to other companies working with it that the once-solid barriers between them become see-through and electronic information is shared as if the companies were one.

Chapter 10. Strengthening the Presentation

Chapter 10. Strengthening the Presentation

Distribution	Distribution is one of the four aspects of marketing. A distribution business is the middleman between the manufacturer and retailer or (usually)in commercial or industrial the business customer.
Personnel	A collective term for all of the employees of an organization. Personnel is also commonly used to refer to the personnel management function or the organizational unit responsible for administering personnel programs.
Jargon	Jargon is terminology, much like slang, that relates to a specific activity, profession, or group. It develops as a kind of shorthand, to express ideas that are frequently discussed between members of a group, and can also have the effect of distinguishing those belonging to a group from those who are not.
Brief	Brief refers to a statement of a party's case or legal arguments, usually prepared by an attorney. Also used to make legal arguments before appellate courts.
Bid	Bid refers to make an offer at an auction or at a judicial sale.
Budget	A financial plan that sets forth management's expectations for revenues and, based on those expectations, allocates the use of specific resources throughout the firm is called budget.
Total cost	The total expense incurred by a firm in producing and marketing a product is the total cost. Total cost is the sum of fixed cost and variable cost. In physical distribution decisions, the sum of all applicable costs for logistical activities.
Buying center	The group of people in an organization who participate in the buying process and share common goals, risks, and knowledge important to a purchase decision is referred to as buying center.
Administrator	Administrator refers to the personal representative appointed by a probate court to settle the estate of a deceased person who died.
Options	Options give the owner the right but not the obligation to buy or sell an underlying security at a set price for a given time period.
Cost-benefit analysis	Cost-benefit analysis refers to a study of the incremental costs and benefits that can be derived from a given course of action.
Return on investment	Return on investment refers to the return a businessperson gets on the money he and other owners invest in the firm; for example, a business that earned $100 on a $1,000 investment would have a ROI of 10 percent: 100 divided by 1000.
Payback	A value that indicates the time period required to recoup an initial investment is a payback. The payback does not include the time-value-of-money concept.
Net present value	Net present value refers to the present value of the cash inflows minus the present value of the cash outflows with the cost of capital used as a discount rate. This method is used to evaluate capital budgeting projects.
Present value	Present value refers to the current or discounted value of a future sum or annuity. The value is discounted back at a given interest rate for a specified time period.
Brand	A name, symbol, or design that identifies the goods or services of one seller or group of sellers and distinguishes them from the goods and services of competitors is a brand.
Premium	Premium refers to the fee charged by an insurance company for an insurance policy. The rate of losses must be relatively predictable: In order to set the premium (prices) insurers must be able to estimate them accurately.
Productivity	Productivity refers to the total output of goods and services in a given period of time divided by work hours.
Depreciation	The systematic write-off of the cost of a tangible asset over its estimated useful life is

Go to Cram101.com for the Practice Tests for this Chapter.

Chapter 10. Strengthening the Presentation

Chapter 10. Strengthening the Presentation

	called depreciation.
Inflation	A general rise in the prices of goods and services over time is an inflation. It is a change in some important measure of money which says either real or apparent value is falling.
Cost of capital	Cost of capital refers to the cost of alternative sources of financing to the firm.
Capital	Contributions of money and other property to a business made by the owners of the business are capital.

Chapter 10. Strengthening the Presentation

Chapter 11. Responding to Objections

Objection	In the trial of a case the formal remonstrance made by counsel to something that has been said or done, in order to obtain the court's ruling thereon is an objection.
Buyer	A buyer refers to a role in the buying center with formal authority and responsibility to select the supplier and negotiate the terms of the contract.
Negotiation	Negotiation is the process whereby interested parties resolve disputes, agree upon courses of action, bargain for individual or collective advantage, and/or attempt to craft outcomes which serve their mutual interests.
Product	Any physical good, service, or idea that satisfies a want or need is called product. Product in project management is a physical entity created as a result of project work.
Interest	Interest refers to the payment the issuer of the bond makes to the bondholders for use of the borrowed money. It is the return to capital achieved over time or as the result of an event.
Customer service	The ability of logistics management to satisfy users in terms of time, dependability, communication, and convenience is called the customer service.
Grant	Grant refers to an intergovernmental transfer of funds. Since the New Deal, state and local governments have become increasingly dependent upon federal grants for an almost infinite variety of programs.
Exhibit	Exhibit refers to a copy of a written instrument on which a pleading is founded, annexed to the pleading and by reference made a part of it. Any paper or thing offered in evidence and marked for identification.
Brand	A name, symbol, or design that identifies the goods or services of one seller or group of sellers and distinguishes them from the goods and services of competitors is a brand.
Customs	Customs is an authority or agency in a country responsible for collecting customs duties and for controlling the flow of people, animals and goods (including personal effects and hazardous items) in and out of the country.
Nonverbal communication	The many additional ways that communication is accomplished beyond the oral or written word is referred to as nonverbal communication.
Communication	Communication refers to the social process in which two or more parties exchange information and share meaning.
Standing	Standing refers to the legal requirement that anyone seeking to challenge a particular action in court must demonstrate that such action substantially affects his legitimate interests before he will be entitled to bring suit.
Personnel	A collective term for all of the employees of an organization. Personnel is also commonly used to refer to the personnel management function or the organizational unit responsible for administering personnel programs.
Grand jury	A grand jury is a type of common law jury responsible for investigating alleged crimes, examining evidence, and issuing indictments if they believe that there is enough evidence for a trial to proceed. A grand jury is distinguished from a petit jury, which is used during trial; the names refer to their respective sizes (typically 25 and 12 members respectively).
Jury	A body of lay persons, selected by lot, or by some other fair and impartial means, to ascertain, under the guidance of the judge, the truth in questions of fact arising either in civil litigation or a criminal process is referred to as jury.
Price fixing	Price fixing refers to a conspiracy among firms to set prices for a product.
Industry	Industry refers to a group of firms offering products that are close substitutes for each other.

Chapter 11. Responding to Objections

Chapter 11. Responding to Objections

Trust	Trust refers to a legal relationship in which a person who has legal title to property has the duty to hold it for the use or benefit of another person. The term is also used in a general sense to mean confidence reposed in one person by another.
Prejudice	Prejudice is, as the name implies, the process of "pre-judging" something. It implies coming to a judgment on a subject before learning where the preponderance of evidence actually lies, or forming a judgment without direct experience.
Dividend	Distribution of profits of the corporation to shareholders is referred to as dividend.
Competition	In business, competition occurs when rival organizations with similar products and services attempt to gain customers.
Inventory	Inventory refers to physical material purchased from suppliers, which may or may not be reworked for sale to customers. A unique element of services-the need for and cost of having a service provider available.
Reciprocity	An industrial buying practice in which two organizations agree to purchase each other's products and services is called reciprocity.
Preparation	Preparation refers to usually the first stage in the creative process. It includes education and formal training.
Empathy	Empathy refers to dimension of service quality-caring individualized attention provided to customers.
Advertising agency	A firm that specializes in the creation, production, and placement of advertising messages and may provide other services that facilitate the marketing communications process is an advertising agency.
Advertising	Advertising refers to paid, nonpersonal communication through various media by organizations and individuals who are in some way identified in the advertising message.
Agency	Agency refers to a legal relationship in which an agent acts under the direction of a principal for the principal's benefit. Also used to refer to government regulatory bodies of all kinds.
Client	The organizations with the products, services, or causes to be marketed and for which advertising agencies and other marketing promotional firms provide services is referred to as a client.
Purchasing	Purchasing refers to the function in a firm that searches for quality material resources, finds the best suppliers, and negotiates the best price for goods and services.
Deception	According to the Federal Trade Commission, a misrepresentation, omission, or practice that is likely to mislead the consumer acting reasonably in the circumstances to the consumer's detriment is referred to as deception.
Options	Options give the owner the right but not the obligation to buy or sell an underlying security at a set price for a given time period.
Discount	A discount is the reduction of the base price of a product.
Production	The creation of finished goods and services using the factors of production: land, labor, capital, entrepreneurship, and knowledge.
Hearing	A hearing is a proceeding before a court or other decision-making body or officer. A hearing is generally distinguished from a trial in that it is usually shorter and often less formal.
Compensation	A payment that is given or recieved as reparation for a service or loss is referred to as compensation.

Chapter 11. Responding to Objections

Chapter 11. Responding to Objections

Stock	In financial terminology, stock is the capital raized by a corporation, through the issuance and sale of shares. A shareholder is any person or organization which owns one or more shares of a corporation's stock. The aggregate value of a corporation's issued shares is its market capitalization.
Testimonial	Testimonial refers to a statement by a public figure professing the merits of some product or service.
Testimony	In some contexts, the word bears the same import as the word evidence, but in most connections it has a much narrower meaning. Testimony are the words heard from the witness in court, and evidence is what the jury considers it worth.
Patent	A patent is a set of exclusive rights granted by a state to a person for a fixed period of time in exchange for the regulated, public disclosure of certain details of a device, method, process or composition of matter which is new, inventive, and useful or industrially applicable.
Coupon	In finance, a coupon is "attached" to bonds, either physically (as with old bonds) or electronically. Each coupon represents a predetermined payment promized to the bond-holder in return for his or her loan of money to the bond-issuer. The bond-holder is typically not the original lender, but receives this payment for effectively lending the money. The coupon rate (the amount promized per dollar of the face value of the bond) helps determine the interest rate or yield on the bond.
Contract	A contract is a "promise" or an "agreement" that is enforced or recognized by the law. In the civil law, contracts are considered to be part of the general law of obligations. This article describes the law relating to contracts in common law jurisdictions.
Manager	A person who is formally responsible for supporting the work efforts of other people is a manager.
Intranet	Intranet refers to a companywide network, closed to public access, that uses Internet-type technology. A set of communications links within one company that travel over the Internet but are closed to public access.
Leverage	Leverage is using given resources in such a way that the potential positive or negative outcome is magnified. In finance, this generally refers to borrowing.
Two-step approach	A direct-marketing strategy in which the first effort is designed to screen or qualify potential buyers, while the second effort has the responsibility of generating the response is called two-step approach.
Cost-benefit analysis	Cost-benefit analysis refers to a study of the incremental costs and benefits that can be derived from a given course of action.
Promotion	Promotion refers to all the techniques sellers use to motivate people to buy products or services. An attempt by marketers to inform people about products and to persuade them to participate in an exchange.
Partnership	In the common law, a partnership is a type of business structure in which partners share with each other the profits or losses of the business undertaking in which they have all invested.
Compromise	Compromise occurs when the interaction is moderately important to meeting goals and the goals are neither completely compatible nor completely incompatible.

Go to **Cram101.com** for the Practice Tests for this Chapter.

Chapter 11. Responding to Objections

Chapter 12. Obtaining Commitment

Closing	The finalization of a real estate sales transaction that passes title to the property from the seller to the buyer is referred to as a closing. Closing is a sales term which refers to the process of making a sale. It refers to reaching the final step, which may be an exchange of money or acquiring a signature.
Objection	In the trial of a case the formal remonstrance made by counsel to something that has been said or done, in order to obtain the court's ruling thereon is an objection.
Consultative selling	Consultative selling focuses on problem definition, where the salesperson serves as an expert on problem recognition and resolution.
Trust	Trust refers to a legal relationship in which a person who has legal title to property has the duty to hold it for the use or benefit of another person. The term is also used in a general sense to mean confidence reposed in one person by another.
Closing techniques	Ways of concluding a sale, including getting a series of small commitments and then asking for the order are called closing techniques.
Buyer	A buyer refers to a role in the buying center with formal authority and responsibility to select the supplier and negotiate the terms of the contract.
Exhibit	Exhibit refers to a copy of a written instrument on which a pleading is founded, annexed to the pleading and by reference made a part of it. Any paper or thing offered in evidence and marked for identification.
Product	Any physical good, service, or idea that satisfies a want or need is called product. Product in project management is a physical entity created as a result of project work.
Discount	A discount is the reduction of the base price of a product.
Options	Options give the owner the right but not the obligation to buy or sell an underlying security at a set price for a given time period.
Corporation	A form of business organization that is owned by owners, called shareholders, who have no inherent right to manage the business, and is managed by a board of directors that is elected by the shareholders is called a corporation.
Reseller	Reseller refers to a wholesaler or retailer that buys physical products and resells them again without any processing.
Quantity discounts	Quantity discounts refer to reductions in unit costs for a larger order.
Quantity discount	A quantity discount is a price reduction given for a large order.
Rebate	Rebate refers to a sales promotion in which money is returned to the consumer based on proof of purchase.
Cash discount	Cash discount refers to a reduction in the invoice price if payment is made within a specified time period.
Warehouse	Warehouse refers to a location, often decentralized, that a firm uses to store, consolidate, age, or mix stock; house product-recall programs; or ease tax burdens.
Inventory	Inventory refers to physical material purchased from suppliers, which may or may not be reworked for sale to customers. A unique element of services-the need for and cost of having a service provider available.
Budget	A financial plan that sets forth management's expectations for revenues and, based on those expectations, allocates the use of specific resources throughout the firm is called budget.

Go to **Cram101.com** for the Practice Tests for this Chapter.

Chapter 12. Obtaining Commitment

Chapter 12. Obtaining Commitment

Total cost	The total expense incurred by a firm in producing and marketing a product is the total cost. Total cost is the sum of fixed cost and variable cost. In physical distribution decisions, the sum of all applicable costs for logistical activities.
Trial	An examination before a competent tribunal, according to the law of the land, of the facts or law put in issue in a cause, for the purpose of determining such issue is a trial. When the court hears and determines any issue of fact or law for the purpose of determining the rights of the parties, it may be considered a trial.
Cooperative advertising	Advertising programs by which a manufacturer pays a percentage of the retailer's local advertising expense for advertising the manufacturer's products are called cooperative advertising.
Cooperative	A business owned and controlled by the people who use it, producers, consumers, or workers with similar needs who pool their resources for mutual gain is called cooperative.
Advertising	Advertising refers to paid, nonpersonal communication through various media by organizations and individuals who are in some way identified in the advertising message.
Layout	Layout refers to the physical arrangement of the various parts of an advertisement including the headline, subheads, illustrations, body copy, and any identifying marks.
Context	The effect of the background under which a message often takes on more and richer meaning is a context. Context is especially important in cross-cultural interactions because some cultures are said to be high context or low context.
Adaptive selling	Adaptive selling refers to a need-satisfaction sales presentation that involves adjusting the presentation to fit the selling situation.
Exchange	The trade of things of value between buyer and seller so that each is better off after the trade is called the exchange.
Stock	In financial terminology, stock is the capital raized by a corporation, through the issuance and sale of shares. A shareholder is any person or organization which owns one or more shares of a corporation's stock. The aggregate value of a corporation's issued shares is its market capitalization.
Promotion	Promotion refers to all the techniques sellers use to motivate people to buy products or services. An attempt by marketers to inform people about products and to persuade them to participate in an exchange.
Vendor	A person who sells property to a vendee is a vendor. The words vendor and vendee are more commonly applied to the seller and purchaser of real estate, and the words seller and buyer are more commonly applied to the seller and purchaser of personal property.
Balance sheet	A balance sheet, in formal bookkeeping and accounting, is a statement of the book value of a business or other organization or person at a particular date, often at the end of its "fiscal year," as distinct from an income statement, also known as a profit and loss account (P&L), which records revenue and expenses over a specified period of time.
Interest	Interest refers to the payment the issuer of the bond makes to the bondholders for use of the borrowed money. It is the return to capital achieved over time or as the result of an event.
Broker	An agent who bargains or carries on negotiations in behalf of the principal as an intermediary between the latter and third persons in transacting business relative to the acquisition of contractual rights, or to the sale or purchase of property the custody of which is not entrusted to him or her for the purpose of discharging the agency is called a broker.
Preference	The act of a debtor in paying or securing one or more of his creditors in a manner more

Chapter 12. Obtaining Commitment

Chapter 12. Obtaining Commitment

	favorable to them than to other creditors or to the exclusion of such other creditors is a preference. In the absence of statute, a preference is perfectly good, but to be legal it must be bona fide, and not a mere subterfuge of the debtor to secure a future benefit to himself or to prevent the application of his property to his debts.
Insurance	A means for persons and businesses to protect themselves against the risk of loss is insurance.
Lease	A contract for the possession and use of land or other property, including goods, on one side, and a recompense of rent or other income on the other is the lease.
Partnership	In the common law, a partnership is a type of business structure in which partners share with each other the profits or losses of the business undertaking in which they have all invested.
Empathy	Empathy refers to dimension of service quality-caring individualized attention provided to customers.
Purchasing	Purchasing refers to the function in a firm that searches for quality material resources, finds the best suppliers, and negotiates the best price for goods and services.
Preparation	Preparation refers to usually the first stage in the creative process. It includes education and formal training.
Action plan	Action plan refers to a written document that includes the steps the trainee and manager will take to ensure that training transfers to the job.

Chapter 12. Obtaining Commitment

Chapter 13. Building Long-term Partnerships

Product	Any physical good, service, or idea that satisfies a want or need is called product. Product in project management is a physical entity created as a result of project work.
Revenue	Revenue refers to the total amount of money a business earns in a given period by selling goods and services. The value of what is received for goods sold, services rendered.
Competitive advantage	A business is said to have a competitive advantage when its unique strengths, often based on cost, quality, time, and innovation, offer consumers a greater percieved value and there by diffetiating it from its competitors.
Contract	A contract is a "promise" or an "agreement" that is enforced or recognized by the law. In the civil law, contracts are considered to be part of the general law of obligations. This article describes the law relating to contracts in common law jurisdictions.
Competition	In business, competition occurs when rival organizations with similar products and services attempt to gain customers.
Bottom line	Bottom line refers to the last line in a profit and loss statement; it refers to net profit.
Exhibit	Exhibit refers to a copy of a written instrument on which a pleading is founded, annexed to the pleading and by reference made a part of it. Any paper or thing offered in evidence and marked for identification.
Total revenue	The total money received from the sale of a product is referred to as the total revenue. It equals the price of the product multiplied by the quantity sold.
Industry	Industry refers to a group of firms offering products that are close substitutes for each other.
Buyer	A buyer refers to a role in the buying center with formal authority and responsibility to select the supplier and negotiate the terms of the contract.
Dissolution	Dissolution is the process of admitting or removing a partner in a partnership.
Trust	Trust refers to a legal relationship in which a person who has legal title to property has the duty to hold it for the use or benefit of another person. The term is also used in a general sense to mean confidence reposed in one person by another.
Partnership	In the common law, a partnership is a type of business structure in which partners share with each other the profits or losses of the business undertaking in which they have all invested.
Vendor	A person who sells property to a vendee is a vendor. The words vendor and vendee are more commonly applied to the seller and purchaser of real estate, and the words seller and buyer are more commonly applied to the seller and purchaser of personal property.
Complaint	The pleading in a civil case in which the plaintiff states his claim and requests relief is called complaint. In the common law, it is a formal legal document that sets out the basic facts and legal reasons that the filing party (the plaintiffs) believes are sufficient to support a claim against another person, persons, entity or entities (the defendants) that entitles the plaintiff(s) to a remedy (either money damages or injunctive relief).
Inventory	Inventory refers to physical material purchased from suppliers, which may or may not be reworked for sale to customers. A unique element of services-the need for and cost of having a service provider available.
Management	Management characterizes the process of leading and directing all or part of an organization, often a business, through the deployment and manipulation of resources. Early twentieth-century management writer Mary Parker Follett defined management as "the art of getting things done through people."
Electronic data	Combine proprietary computer and telecommunication technologies to exchange electronic

Chapter 13. Building Long-term Partnerships

Chapter 13. Building Long-term Partnerships

interchange	invoices, payments, and information among suppliers, manufacturers, and retailers is referred to as the electronic data interchange.
Productivity	Productivity refers to the total output of goods and services in a given period of time divided by work hours.
Purchasing	Purchasing refers to the function in a firm that searches for quality material resources, finds the best suppliers, and negotiates the best price for goods and services.
Communication	Communication refers to the social process in which two or more parties exchange information and share meaning.
Supply chain management	The integration and organization of information and logistic activities across firms in a supply chain for the purpose of creating and delivering goods and services that provide value to customers is supply chain management.
Supply chain	The sequence of linked activities that must be performed by various organizations to move goods from the sources of raw materials to ultimate consumers is referred to as supply chain.
Customer service	The ability of logistics management to satisfy users in terms of time, dependability, communication, and convenience is called the customer service.
Product manager	Product manager refers to a person who plans, implements, and controls the annual and long-range plans for the products for which he or she is responsible.
Manager	A person who is formally responsible for supporting the work efforts of other people is a manager.
Specialty advertising	An advertising, sales promotion, and motivational communications medium that employs useful articles of merchandise imprinted with an advertiser's name, message, or logo is referred to as specialty advertising.
Advertising	Advertising refers to paid, nonpersonal communication through various media by organizations and individuals who are in some way identified in the advertising message.
Bribery	When one person gives another person money, property, favors, or anything else of value for a favor in return, we have bribery. Often referred to as a payoff or 'kickback.'
Stock	In financial terminology, stock is the capital raized by a corporation, through the issuance and sale of shares. A shareholder is any person or organization which owns one or more shares of a corporation's stock. The aggregate value of a corporation's issued shares is its market capitalization.
Client	The organizations with the products, services, or causes to be marketed and for which advertising agencies and other marketing promotional firms provide services is referred to as a client.
Customer contact	Customer contact refers to a characteristic of services that notes that customers tend to be more involved in the production of services than they are in manufactured goods.
Strategic partnership	Strategic partnership refers to an association between two firms by which they agree to work together to achieve a strategic goal. This is often associated with long-term supplier-customer relationships.
Mistake	In contract law a mistake is incorrect understanding by one or more parties to a contract and may be used as grounds to invalidate the agreement. Common law has identified three different types of mistake in contract: unilateral mistake, mutual mistake, and common mistake.
Public relations	Public relations refers to the management function that evaluates public attitudes, changes policies and procedures in response to the public's requests, and executes a program of action and information to earn public understanding and acceptance.

Go to **Cram101.com** for the Practice Tests for this Chapter.

Chapter 13. Building Long-term Partnerships

Chapter 13. Building Long-term Partnerships

Authority	Authority in agency law, refers to an agent's ability to affect his principal's legal relations with third parties. Also used to refer to an actor's legal power or ability to do something. In addition, sometimes used to refer to a statute, case, or other legal source that justifies a particular result.
Grievance	A charge by employees that management is not abiding by the terms of the negotiated labormanagement agreement is the grievance.
Policy	Similar to a script in that a policy can be a less than completely rational decision-making method. Involves the use of a pre-existing set of decision steps for any problem that presents itself.
Holding	The holding is a court's determination of a matter of law based on the issue presented in the particular case. In other words: under this law, with these facts, this result.
Technical analysis	Uses price and volume data to determine past trends, which are expected to continue into the future is called technical analysis.
Appeal	Appeal refers to the act of asking an appellate court to overturn a decision after the trial court's final judgment has been entered.
Comprehensive	A comprehensive refers to a layout accurate in size, color, scheme, and other necessary details to show how a final ad will look. For presentation only, never for reproduction.
Corporation	A form of business organization that is owned by owners, called shareholders, who have no inherent right to manage the business, and is managed by a board of directors that is elected by the shareholders is called a corporation.
Users	Users refer to people in the organization who actually use the product or service purchased by the buying center.
Interest	Interest refers to the payment the issuer of the bond makes to the bondholders for use of the borrowed money. It is the return to capital achieved over time or as the result of an event.
Current account	The net balance of a country's international payment stemming from exports and imports of goods and services along with unilateral transfers (gifts and foreign aid) is referred to as a current account.
Sales promotion	Sales promotion refers to the promotional tool that stimulates consumer purchasing and dealer interest by means of short-term activities.
Promotion	Promotion refers to all the techniques sellers use to motivate people to buy products or services. An attempt by marketers to inform people about products and to persuade them to participate in an exchange.
Marketing	The American Marketing Association suggests that Marketing is "the process of planning and executing the pricing, promotion, and distribution of goods, ideas, and services to create exchanges that satisfy individual and organizational goals."
Honor	Payment of a drawer's properly drawn check by the drawee bank is referred to as honor.
Layout	Layout refers to the physical arrangement of the various parts of an advertisement including the headline, subheads, illustrations, body copy, and any identifying marks.
Reseller	Reseller refers to a wholesaler or retailer that buys physical products and resells them again without any processing.
Trade show	A type of exhibition or forum where manufacturers can display their products to current as well as prospective buyers is referred to as trade show.
Hearing	A hearing is a proceeding before a court or other decision-making body or officer. A hearing is generally distinguished from a trial in that it is usually shorter and often less formal.

Go to **Cram101.com** for the Practice Tests for this Chapter.

Chapter 13. Building Long-term Partnerships

Chapter 13. Building Long-term Partnerships

Buying center	The group of people in an organization who participate in the buying process and share common goals, risks, and knowledge important to a purchase decision is referred to as buying center.
Credibility	The extent to which a source is perceived as having knowledge, skill, or experience relevant to a communication topic and can be trusted to give an unbiased opinion or present objective information on the issue is called credibility.
Total Quality Management	The practice of striving for customer satisfaction by ensuring quality from all departments in an organization is called total quality management.
Quality management	Quality management is a method for ensuring that all the activities necessary to design, develop and implement a product or service are effective and efficient with respect to the system and its performance.
Continuous improvement	Constantly improving the way the organization does things so that customer needs can be better satisfied is referred to as continuous improvement.
Voice of the customer	A term that refers to the wants, opinions, perceptions, and desires of the customer is a voice of the customer.
Pledge	In law a pledge (also pawn) is a bailment of personal property as a security for some debt or engagement.
Bid	Bid refers to make an offer at an auction or at a judicial sale.
Discount	A discount is the reduction of the base price of a product.
Expense	An expense refers to costs involved in operating a business, such as rent, utilities, and salaries.
Organizational culture	Widely shared values within an organization that provide coherence and cooperation to achieve common goals are referred to as a organizational culture.
Channel	Channel, in communications (sometimes called communications channel), refers to the medium used to convey information from a sender (or transmitter) to a receiver.
Loyalty	Marketers tend to define customer loyalty as making repeat purchases. Some argue that it should be defined attitudinally as a strongly positive feeling about the brand.
Administration	Administration refers to the management and direction of the affairs of governments and institutions; a collective term for all policymaking officials of a government; the execution and implementation of public policy.
Production	The creation of finished goods and services using the factors of production: land, labor, capital, entrepreneurship, and knowledge.
Corporate culture	The whole collection of beliefs, values, and behaviors of a firm that send messages to those within and outside the company about how business is done is the corporate culture.
Assessment	Collecting information and providing feedback to employees about their behavior, communication style, or skills is an assessment.
Distribution	Distribution is one of the four aspects of marketing. A distribution business is the middleman between the manufacturer and retailer or (usually)in commercial or industrial the business customer.
Change agent	A change agent is someone who engages either deliberately or whose behavior results in social, cultural or behavioral change. This can be studied scientifically and effective techniques can be discovered and employed.
Agent	One who acts under the direction of a principal for the principal's benefit in a legal relationship known as agency is called agent.

Chapter 13. Building Long-term Partnerships

Chapter 13. Building Long-term Partnerships

Cross-functional team	That which brings together persons from different functions to work on a common task is called a cross-functional team.
Resistance to change	Resistance to change refers to an attitude or behavior that shows unwillingness to make or support a change.
Positioning	The art and science of fitting the product or service to one or more segments of the market in such a way as to set it meaningfully apart from competition is called positioning.
Mass marketing	Mass marketing refers to developing products and promotions to please large groups of people.
Marketing research	Marketing research refers to the analysis of markets to determine opportunities and challenges, and to find the information needed to make good decisions.
Marketing management	Marketing management refers to the process of planning and executing the conception, pricing, promotion, and distribution of ideas, goods, and services to create mutually beneficial exchanges.
Personnel	A collective term for all of the employees of an organization. Personnel is also commonly used to refer to the personnel management function or the organizational unit responsible for administering personnel programs.
Value-added	A customer-based perspective on quality that is used by services, manufacturing, and public sector organizations is value-added. The concept of value-added involves a subjective assessment of the efficacy of every step in the process for the customer.
Insurance	A means for persons and businesses to protect themselves against the risk of loss is insurance.
Advertising agency	A firm that specializes in the creation, production, and placement of advertising messages and may provide other services that facilitate the marketing communications process is an advertising agency.
Agency	Agency refers to a legal relationship in which an agent acts under the direction of a principal for the principal's benefit. Also used to refer to government regulatory bodies of all kinds.
Account executive	The individual who serves as the liaison between the advertising agency and the client is the account executive. The account executive is responsible for managing all of the services the agency provides to the client and representing the agency's point of view to the client.
Audit	Audit refers to the verification of a company's books and records pursuant to federal securities laws, state laws, and stock exchange rules that must be performed by an independent CPA.

Go to **Cram101.com** for the Practice Tests for this Chapter.

Chapter 13. Building Long-term Partnerships

Chapter 14. Formal Negotiating

Buyer	A buyer refers to a role in the buying center with formal authority and responsibility to select the supplier and negotiate the terms of the contract.
Negotiation	Negotiation is the process whereby interested parties resolve disputes, agree upon courses of action, bargain for individual or collective advantage, and/or attempt to craft outcomes which serve their mutual interests.
Tactic	A short-term immediate decision that, in its totality, leads to the achievement of strategic goals is called a tactic.
Discount	A discount is the reduction of the base price of a product.
Compensation	A payment that is given or recieved as reparation for a service or loss is referred to as compensation.
Negotiable	A negotiable instrument is one that can be bought and sold after being issued - in other words, it is a tradable instrument.
Production	The creation of finished goods and services using the factors of production: land, labor, capital, entrepreneurship, and knowledge.
Marketing	The American Marketing Association suggests that Marketing is "the process of planning and executing the pricing, promotion, and distribution of goods, ideas, and services to create exchanges that satisfy individual and organizational goals."
Human resources	Human resources refers to the individuals within the firm, and to the portion of the firm's organization that deals with hiring, firing, training, and other personnel issues.
Accounting	The recording, classifying, summarizing, and interpreting of financial events and transactions to provide management and other interested parties the information they need to make good decisions is called accounting.
Purchasing	Purchasing refers to the function in a firm that searches for quality material resources, finds the best suppliers, and negotiates the best price for goods and services.
Exhibit	Exhibit refers to a copy of a written instrument on which a pleading is founded, annexed to the pleading and by reference made a part of it. Any paper or thing offered in evidence and marked for identification.
Preparation	Preparation refers to usually the first stage in the creative process. It includes education and formal training.
Product	Any physical good, service, or idea that satisfies a want or need is called product. Product in project management is a physical entity created as a result of project work.
Exchange	The trade of things of value between buyer and seller so that each is better off after the trade is called the exchange.
Mentor	An experienced employee who supervises, coaches, and guides lower-level employees by introducing them to the right people and generally being their organizational sponsor is a mentor.
Manager	A person who is formally responsible for supporting the work efforts of other people is a manager.
Interpersonal skills	Interpersonal skills are used to communicate with, understand, and motivate individuals and groups.
Premium	Premium refers to the fee charged by an insurance company for an insurance policy. The rate of losses must be relatively predictable: In order to set the premium (prices) insurers must be able to estimate them accurately.

Go to **Cram101.com** for the Practice Tests for this Chapter.

Chapter 14. Formal Negotiating

Chapter 14. Formal Negotiating

Brainstorming	Brainstorming refers to a technique designed to overcome our natural tendency to evaluate and criticize ideas and thereby reduce the creative output of those ideas. People are encouraged to produce ideas/options without criticizing, often at a very fast pace to minimize our natural tendency to criticize.
Mistake	In contract law a mistake is incorrect understanding by one or more parties to a contract and may be used as grounds to invalidate the agreement. Common law has identified three different types of mistake in contract: unilateral mistake, mutual mistake, and common mistake.
Management	Management characterizes the process of leading and directing all or part of an organization, often a business, through the deployment and manipulation of resources. Early twentieth-century management writer Mary Parker Follett defined management as "the art of getting things done through people."
Cooperative	A business owned and controlled by the people who use it, producers, consumers, or workers with similar needs who pool their resources for mutual gain is called cooperative.
Contract	A contract is a "promise" or an "agreement" that is enforced or recognized by the law. In the civil law, contracts are considered to be part of the general law of obligations. This article describes the law relating to contracts in common law jurisdictions.
Options	Options give the owner the right but not the obligation to buy or sell an underlying security at a set price for a given time period.
Layout	Layout refers to the physical arrangement of the various parts of an advertisement including the headline, subheads, illustrations, body copy, and any identifying marks.
Remainder	A remainder in property law is a future interest created in a transferee that is capable of becoming possessory upon the natural termination of a prior estate created by the same instrument.
Standing	Standing refers to the legal requirement that anyone seeking to challenge a particular action in court must demonstrate that such action substantially affects his legitimate interests before he will be entitled to bring suit.
Staffing	Staffing refers to a management function that includes hiring, motivating, and retaining the best people available to accomplish the company's objectives.
Abandonment	Abandonment in law, the relinquishment of an interest, claim, privilege or possession. This broad meaning has a number of applications in different branches of law.
Expense	An expense refers to costs involved in operating a business, such as rent, utilities, and salaries.
Insurance	A means for persons and businesses to protect themselves against the risk of loss is insurance.
Grant	Grant refers to an intergovernmental transfer of funds . Since the New Deal, state and local governments have become increasingly dependent upon federal grants for an almost infinite variety of programs.
Appeal	Appeal refers to the act of asking an appellate court to overturn a decision after the trial court's final judgment has been entered.
Budget	A financial plan that sets forth management's expectations for revenues and, based on those expectations, allocates the use of specific resources throughout the firm is called budget.
Unions	Employee organizations that have the main goal of representing members in employee-management bargaining over job-related issues are called unions.
Union	A union refers to employee organizations that have the main goal of representing members in

Chapter 14. Formal Negotiating

	employeemanagement bargaining over job-related issues.
Formal contract	Formal contract refers to a contract that requires a special form or method of creation.
Partnership	In the common law, a partnership is a type of business structure in which partners share with each other the profits or losses of the business undertaking in which they have all invested.

Chapter 14. Formal Negotiating

Chapter 15. Selling to Resellers

Reseller	Reseller refers to a wholesaler or retailer that buys physical products and resells them again without any processing.
Distribution	Distribution is one of the four aspects of marketing. A distribution business is the middleman between the manufacturer and retailer or (usually)in commercial or industrial the business customer.
End user	End user refers to the ultimate user of a product or service.
Exhibit	Exhibit refers to a copy of a written instrument on which a pleading is founded, annexed to the pleading and by reference made a part of it. Any paper or thing offered in evidence and marked for identification.
Channel	Channel, in communications (sometimes called communications channel), refers to the medium used to convey information from a sender (or transmitter) to a receiver.
Users	Users refer to people in the organization who actually use the product or service purchased by the buying center.
Product	Any physical good, service, or idea that satisfies a want or need is called product. Product in project management is a physical entity created as a result of project work.
Advertising	Advertising refers to paid, nonpersonal communication through various media by organizations and individuals who are in some way identified in the advertising message.
Marketing	The American Marketing Association suggests that Marketing is "the process of planning and executing the pricing, promotion, and distribution of goods, ideas, and services to create exchanges that satisfy individual and organizational goals."
Distribution center	Designed to facilitate the timely movement of goods and represent a very important part of a supply chain is a distribution center.
Warehouse	Warehouse refers to a location, often decentralized, that a firm uses to store, consolidate, age, or mix stock; house product-recall programs; or ease tax burdens.
Breaking bulk	The division or separation of the contents of a package or container is breaking bulk.
Holding	The holding is a court's determination of a matter of law based on the issue presented in the particular case. In other words: under this law, with these facts, this result.
Inventory	Inventory refers to physical material purchased from suppliers, which may or may not be reworked for sale to customers. A unique element of services-the need for and cost of having a service provider available.
Stock keeping unit	Stock keeping unit refers to a unique identification number that defines an item for ordering or inventory purposes.
Stock	In financial terminology, stock is the capital raized by a corporation, through the issuance and sale of shares. A shareholder is any person or organization which owns one or more shares of a corporation's stock. The aggregate value of a corporation's issued shares is its market capitalization.
Discount	A discount is the reduction of the base price of a product.
Brand	A name, symbol, or design that identifies the goods or services of one seller or group of sellers and distinguishes them from the goods and services of competitors is a brand.
Return on investment	Return on investment refers to the return a businessperson gets on the money he and other owners invest in the firm; for example, a business that earned $100 on a $1,000 investment would have a ROI of 10 percent: 100 divided by 1000.
Production	The creation of finished goods and services using the factors of production: land, labor,

Go to Cram101.com for the Practice Tests for this Chapter.

Chapter 15. Selling to Resellers

Chapter 15. Selling to Resellers

	capital, entrepreneurship, and knowledge.
Estate	An estate is the totality of the legal rights, interests, entitlements and obligations attaching to property. In the context of wills and probate, it refers to the totality of the property which the deceased owned or in which some interest was held.
Gross margin	How much a firm earned by buying and selling merchandise is a gross margin. It is an ambiguous phrase that expresses the relationship between gross profit and sales revenue.
Margin	A deposit by a buyer in stocks with a seller or a stockbroker, as security to cover fluctuations in the market in reference to stocks that the buyer has purchased but for which he has not paid is a margin. Commodities are also traded on margin.
Remainder	A remainder in property law is a future interest created in a transferee that is capable of becoming possessory upon the natural termination of a prior estate created by the same instrument.
Interest	Interest refers to the payment the issuer of the bond makes to the bondholders for use of the borrowed money. It is the return to capital achieved over time or as the result of an event.
Revenue	Revenue refers to the total amount of money a business earns in a given period by selling goods and services. The value of what is received for goods sold, services rendered.
Cost of goods sold	A measure of the cost of merchandise sold or cost of raw materials and supplies used for producing items for resale is called cost of goods sold.
Markup	Markup is a term used in marketing to indicate how much the price of a product is above the cost of producing and distributing the product.
Quantity discounts	Quantity discounts refer to reductions in unit costs for a larger order.
Quantity discount	A quantity discount is a price reduction given for a large order.
Expense	An expense refers to costs involved in operating a business, such as rent, utilities, and salaries.
Asset	In business and accounting an asset is anything owned which can produce future economic benefit, whether in possession or by right to take possession, by a person or a group acting together, e.g. a company, the measurement of which can be expressed in monetary terms. Asset is listed on the balance sheet. It has a normal balance of debit.
Vendor	A person who sells property to a vendee is a vendor. The words vendor and vendee are more commonly applied to the seller and purchaser of real estate, and the words seller and buyer are more commonly applied to the seller and purchaser of personal property.
Mistake	In contract law a mistake is incorrect understanding by one or more parties to a contract and may be used as grounds to invalidate the agreement. Common law has identified three different types of mistake in contract: unilateral mistake, mutual mistake, and common mistake.
Premium	Premium refers to the fee charged by an insurance company for an insurance policy. The rate of losses must be relatively predictable: In order to set the premium (prices) insurers must be able to estimate them accurately.
Buyer	A buyer refers to a role in the buying center with formal authority and responsibility to select the supplier and negotiate the terms of the contract.
Appeal	Appeal refers to the act of asking an appellate court to overturn a decision after the trial court's final judgment has been entered.
Trust	Trust refers to a legal relationship in which a person who has legal title to property has

Go to **Cram101.com** for the Practice Tests for this Chapter.

Chapter 15. Selling to Resellers

Chapter 15. Selling to Resellers

	the duty to hold it for the use or benefit of another person. The term is also used in a general sense to mean confidence reposed in one person by another.
Competition	In business, competition occurs when rival organizations with similar products and services attempt to gain customers.
Supply chain	The sequence of linked activities that must be performed by various organizations to move goods from the sources of raw materials to ultimate consumers is referred to as supply chain.
Quick response	An inventory management system designed to reduce the retailer's lead-time, thereby lowering its inventory investment, improving customer service levels, and reducing logistics expense is referred to as quick response.
Electronic data interchange	Combine proprietary computer and telecommunication technologies to exchange electronic invoices, payments, and information among suppliers, manufacturers, and retailers is referred to as the electronic data interchange.
Fixture	Fixture refers to a thing that was originally personal property and that has been actually or constructively affixed to the soil itself or to some structure legally a part of the land.
Industry	Industry refers to a group of firms offering products that are close substitutes for each other.
Retailing	All activities involved in selling, renting, and providing goods and services to ultimate consumers for personal, family, or household use is referred to as retailing.
Derived demand	Derived demand refers to demand for industrial products and services driven by, or derived from, demand for consumer products and services.
Promotion	Promotion refers to all the techniques sellers use to motivate people to buy products or services. An attempt by marketers to inform people about products and to persuade them to participate in an exchange.
Automation	Automation allows machines to do work previously accomplished by people.
Market share	The ratio of sales revenue of the firm to the total sales revenue of all firms in the industry, including the firm itself is the market share.
Marketing research	Marketing research refers to the analysis of markets to determine opportunities and challenges, and to find the information needed to make good decisions.
Allowance	An allowance is an amount of money provided to employees to offset specific expenses such as for travel interstate or to buy protective clothing
Trade discounts	Trade discounts refer to price reductions to reward wholesalers or retailers for marketing functions they will perform in the future.
Promotional allowance	Promotional allowance refers to cash payment or extra amount of 'free goods' awarded sellers in the channel of distribution for undertaking certain advertising or selling activities to promote a product.
Cooperative advertising	Advertising programs by which a manufacturer pays a percentage of the retailer's local advertising expense for advertising the manufacturer's products are called cooperative advertising.
Cooperative	A business owned and controlled by the people who use it, producers, consumers, or workers with similar needs who pool their resources for mutual gain is called cooperative.
Forward buying	Forward buying refers to a response to discounts offered by manufacturers in which retailers purchase more merchandise than they plan to sell during the promotion. The remaining stock is sold at a regular price later, or diverted to another store.

Go to **Cram101.com** for the Practice Tests for this Chapter.

Chapter 15. Selling to Resellers

Chapter 15. Selling to Resellers

Consignment	Consignment refers to a bailment for sale. The consignee does not undertake the absolute obligation to sell or pay for the goods.
Financial risk	The risk related to the inability of the firm to meet its debt obligations as they come due is called financial risk.
Letter of credit	An instrument containing a request to pay to the bearer or person named money, or sell him or her some commodity on credit or give something of value and look to the drawer of the letter for recompense is called letter of credit.
Level of service	The degree of service provided to the customer by self, limited, and full-service retailers is referred to as the level of service.
Innovation	The process of creating and doing new things that are introduced into the marketplace as products, processes, or services is innovation.
Management	Management characterizes the process of leading and directing all or part of an organization, often a business, through the deployment and manipulation of resources. Early twentieth-century management writer Mary Parker Follett defined management as "the art of getting things done through people."
Customer service	The ability of logistics management to satisfy users in terms of time, dependability, communication, and convenience is called the customer service.
Partnership	In the common law, a partnership is a type of business structure in which partners share with each other the profits or losses of the business undertaking in which they have all invested.
Lease	A contract for the possession and use of land or other property, including goods, on one side, and a recompense of rent or other income on the other is the lease.
Specialty advertising	An advertising, sales promotion, and motivational communications medium that employs useful articles of merchandise imprinted with an advertiser's name, message, or logo is referred to as specialty advertising.
Trade show	A type of exhibition or forum where manufacturers can display their products to current as well as prospective buyers is referred to as trade show.
Closing	The finalization of a real estate sales transaction that passes title to the property from the seller to the buyer is referred to as a closing. Closing is a sales term which refers to the process of making a sale. It refers to reaching the final step, which may be an exchange of money or acquiring a signature.
Sweepstakes	Sales promotions consisting of a game of chance requiring no analytical or creative effort by the consumer is a sweepstakes.
Coupon	In finance, a coupon is "attached" to bonds, either physically (as with old bonds) or electronically. Each coupon represents a predetermined payment promized to the bond-holder in return for his or her loan of money to the bond-issuer. The bond-holder is typically not the original lender, but receives this payment for effectively lending the money. The coupon rate (the amount promized per dollar of the face value of the bond) helps determine the interest rate or yield on the bond.
Pull strategy	Promotional strategy in which heavy advertising and sales promotion efforts are directed toward consumers so that they'll request the products from retailers is called pull strategy.
Advertisement	Advertisement is the promotion of goods, services, companies and ideas, usually by an identified sponsor. Marketers see advertising as part of an overall promotional strategy.
Participation	Participation refers to the process of giving employees a voice in making decisions about their own work.

Chapter 15. Selling to Resellers

Point-of-purchase displays	Product displays taking the form of advertising signs, which sometimes actually hold or display the product, and are often located in high-traffic areas near the cash register on the end of an aisle are called point-of-purchase displays.
Push strategy	Promotional strategy in which the producer uses advertising, personal selling, sales promotion, and all other promotional tools to convince wholesalers and retailers to stock and sell merchandise is called push strategy.
Incentive	A reward offered by a marketer to a prospective customer in return for furnishing information or making a purchase is referred to as an incentive.
Personal selling	Personal selling is interpersonal communication, often face to face, between a sales representative and an individual or group, usually with the objective of making a sale.
Push money	Cash payments made directly to the retailers' or wholesalers' sales force to encourage them to promote and sell a manufacturer's product are called push money.
Category management	An organizational system whereby managers have responsibility for the marketing programs for a particular category or line of products is a category management.
Logistics	Those activities that focus on getting the right amount of the right products to the right place at the right time at the lowest possible cost is referred to as logistics.
Communication channel	The pathways through which messages are communicated are called a communication channel.
Communication	Communication refers to the social process in which two or more parties exchange information and share meaning.

Go to **Cram101.com** for the Practice Tests for this Chapter.

Chapter 16. Managing Your Time and Territory

Insurance	A means for persons and businesses to protect themselves against the risk of loss is insurance.
Management	Management characterizes the process of leading and directing all or part of an organization, often a business, through the deployment and manipulation of resources. Early twentieth-century management writer Mary Parker Follett defined management as "the art of getting things done through people."
Product	Any physical good, service, or idea that satisfies a want or need is called product. Product in project management is a physical entity created as a result of project work.
Exhibit	Exhibit refers to a copy of a written instrument on which a pleading is founded, annexed to the pleading and by reference made a part of it. Any paper or thing offered in evidence and marked for identification.
Revenue	Revenue refers to the total amount of money a business earns in a given period by selling goods and services. The value of what is received for goods sold, services rendered.
Conversion	Conversion refers to any distinct act of dominion wrongfully exerted over another's personal property in denial of or inconsistent with his rights therein. That tort committed by a person who deals with chattels not belonging to him in a manner that is inconsistent with the ownership of the lawful owner.
Closing	The finalization of a real estate sales transaction that passes title to the property from the seller to the buyer is referred to as a closing. Closing is a sales term which refers to the process of making a sale. It refers to reaching the final step, which may be an exchange of money or acquiring a signature.
Benchmarking	Discovering how others do something better than your own firm so you can imitate or leapfrog competition is called benchmarking.
Conversion ratio	Conversion ratio refers to the number of shares of common stock an investor will receive if he or she exchanges a convertible bond or convertible preferred stock for common stock.
Yield	The interest rate that equates a future value or an annuity to a given present value is a yield.
Trial	An examination before a competent tribunal, according to the law of the land, of the facts or law put in issue in a cause, for the purpose of determining such issue is a trial. When the court hears and determines any issue of fact or law for the purpose of determining the rights of the parties, it may be considered a trial.
Marketing	The American Marketing Association suggests that Marketing is "the process of planning and executing the pricing, promotion, and distribution of goods, ideas, and services to create exchanges that satisfy individual and organizational goals."
Dividend	Distribution of profits of the corporation to shareholders is referred to as dividend.
Market segments	Market segments refer to the groups that result from the process of market segmentation; these groups ideally have common needs and will respond similarly to a marketing action.
Warrant	A warrant is a security that entitles the holder to buy or sell a certain additional quantity of an underlying security at an agreed-upon price, at the holder's discretion.
Users	Users refer to people in the organization who actually use the product or service purchased by the buying center.
Capital	Contributions of money and other property to a business made by the owners of the business are capital.
Evaluation	The consumer's appraisal of the product or brand on important attributes is called

Chapter 16. Managing Your Time and Territory

Chapter 16. Managing Your Time and Territory

	evaluation.
Brand	A name, symbol, or design that identifies the goods or services of one seller or group of sellers and distinguishes them from the goods and services of competitors is a brand.
Budget	A financial plan that sets forth management's expectations for revenues and, based on those expectations, allocates the use of specific resources throughout the firm is called budget.
Contract	A contract is a "promise" or an "agreement" that is enforced or recognized by the law. In the civil law, contracts are considered to be part of the general law of obligations. This article describes the law relating to contracts in common law jurisdictions.
Industry	Industry refers to a group of firms offering products that are close substitutes for each other.
Market share	The ratio of sales revenue of the firm to the total sales revenue of all firms in the industry, including the firm itself is the market share.
Buyer	A buyer refers to a role in the buying center with formal authority and responsibility to select the supplier and negotiate the terms of the contract.
Verification	Verification refers to the final stage of the creative process where the validity or truthfulness of the insight is determined. The feedback portion of communication in which the receiver sends a message to the source indicating receipt of the message and the degree to which he or she understood the message.
Personnel	A collective term for all of the employees of an organization. Personnel is also commonly used to refer to the personnel management function or the organizational unit responsible for administering personnel programs.
Automation	Automation allows machines to do work previously accomplished by people.
Communication	Communication refers to the social process in which two or more parties exchange information and share meaning.
Competition	In business, competition occurs when rival organizations with similar products and services attempt to gain customers.
Organization chart	Organization chart refers to a visual device, which shows the relationship and divides the organization's work; it shows who is accountable for the completion of specific work and who reports to whom.
Manager	A person who is formally responsible for supporting the work efforts of other people is a manager.
Knowledge base	Knowledge base refers to a database that includes decision rules for use of the data, which may be qualitative as well as quantitative.
Zoning	Government restrictions on the use of private property in order to ensure the orderly growth and development of a community and to protect the health, safety, and welfare of citizens is called zoning.
Brief	Brief refers to a statement of a party's case or legal arguments, usually prepared by an attorney. Also used to make legal arguments before appellate courts.
Productivity	Productivity refers to the total output of goods and services in a given period of time divided by work hours.
Interest	Interest refers to the payment the issuer of the bond makes to the bondholders for use of the borrowed money. It is the return to capital achieved over time or as the result of an event.
Corporation	A form of business organization that is owned by owners, called shareholders, who have no

Chapter 16. Managing Your Time and Territory

Chapter 16. Managing Your Time and Territory

	inherent right to manage the business, and is managed by a board of directors that is elected by the shareholders is called a corporation.
Expense	An expense refers to costs involved in operating a business, such as rent, utilities, and salaries.
Competitive advantage	A business is said to have a competitive advantage when its unique strengths, often based on cost, quality, time, and innovation, offer consumers a greater percieved value and there by differtiating it from its competitors.
Broker	An agent who bargains or carries on negotiations in behalf of the principal as an intermediary between the latter and third persons in transacting business relative to the acquisition of contractual rights, or to the sale or purchase of property the custody of which is not entrusted to him or her for the purpose of discharging the agency is called a broker.
Product line	A group of products that are physically similar or are intended for a similar market are called the product line.
Small business	Small business refers to a business that is independently owned and operated, is not dominant in its field of operation, and meets certain standards of size in terms of employees or annual receipts.

Chapter 16. Managing Your Time and Territory

Chapter 17. Managing Within Your Company

Product	Any physical good, service, or idea that satisfies a want or need is called product. Product in project management is a physical entity created as a result of project work.
Manager	A person who is formally responsible for supporting the work efforts of other people is a manager.
Warehouse	Warehouse refers to a location, often decentralized, that a firm uses to store, consolidate, age, or mix stock; house product-recall programs; or ease tax burdens.
Authority	Authority in agency law, refers to an agent's ability to affect his principal's legal relations with third parties. Also used to refer to an actor's legal power or ability to do something. In addition, sometimes used to refer to a statute, case, or other legal source that justifies a particular result.
Production	The creation of finished goods and services using the factors of production: land, labor, capital, entrepreneurship, and knowledge.
Corporation	A form of business organization that is owned by owners, called shareholders, who have no inherent right to manage the business, and is managed by a board of directors that is elected by the shareholders is called a corporation.
Learning organization	A firm, which values continuous learning and is consistently looking to adapt and change with its environment is referred to as learning organization.
Customer contact	Customer contact refers to a characteristic of services that notes that customers tend to be more involved in the production of services than they are in manufactured goods.
Personnel	A collective term for all of the employees of an organization. Personnel is also commonly used to refer to the personnel management function or the organizational unit responsible for administering personnel programs.
Voice of the customer	A term that refers to the wants, opinions, perceptions, and desires of the customer is a voice of the customer.
Partnership	In the common law, a partnership is a type of business structure in which partners share with each other the profits or losses of the business undertaking in which they have all invested.
Exhibit	Exhibit refers to a copy of a written instrument on which a pleading is founded, annexed to the pleading and by reference made a part of it. Any paper or thing offered in evidence and marked for identification.
Incentive	A reward offered by a marketer to a prospective customer in return for furnishing information or making a purchase is referred to as an incentive.
Communication	Communication refers to the social process in which two or more parties exchange information and share meaning.
Internal customer	An individuals or unit within the firm that receives services from other entities within the organization is an internal customer.
Active listening	Active listening is a way of "listening for meaning" in which the listener checks with the speaker to see that a statement has been correctly heard and understood. The goal of active listening is to improve mutual understanding.
Customer service	The ability of logistics management to satisfy users in terms of time, dependability, communication, and convenience is called the customer service.
External customers	Dealers, who buy products to sell to others, and ultimate customers, who buy products for their own personal use are referred to as external customers.
Policy	Similar to a script in that a policy can be a less than completely rational decision-making method. Involves the use of a pre-existing set of decision steps for any problem that

Chapter 17. Managing Within Your Company

Chapter 17. Managing Within Your Company

	presents itself.
Negotiation	Negotiation is the process whereby interested parties resolve disputes, agree upon courses of action, bargain for individual or collective advantage, and/or attempt to craft outcomes which serve their mutual interests.
Coordination	Coordination refers to the set of mechanisms used in an organization to link the actions of its subunits into a consistent pattern.
Management	Management characterizes the process of leading and directing all or part of an organization, often a business, through the deployment and manipulation of resources. Early twentieth-century management writer Mary Parker Follett defined management as "the art of getting things done through people."
Administration	Administration refers to the management and direction of the affairs of governments and institutions; a collective term for all policymaking officials of a government; the execution and implementation of public policy.
Marketing	The American Marketing Association suggests that Marketing is "the process of planning and executing the pricing, promotion, and distribution of goods, ideas, and services to create exchanges that satisfy individual and organizational goals."
Client	The organizations with the products, services, or causes to be marketed and for which advertising agencies and other marketing promotional firms provide services is referred to as a client.
Competitive advantage	A business is said to have a competitive advantage when its unique strengths, often based on cost, quality, time, and innovation, offer consumers a greater percieved value and there by differtiating it from its competitors.
Promotion	Promotion refers to all the techniques sellers use to motivate people to buy products or services. An attempt by marketers to inform people about products and to persuade them to participate in an exchange.
Compensation	A payment that is given or recieved as reparation for a service or loss is referred to as compensation.
Grant	Grant refers to an intergovernmental transfer of funds . Since the New Deal, state and local governments have become increasingly dependent upon federal grants for an almost infinite variety of programs.
Trial	An examination before a competent tribunal, according to the law of the land, of the facts or law put in issue in a cause, for the purpose of determining such issue is a trial. When the court hears and determines any issue of fact or law for the purpose of determining the rights of the parties, it may be considered a trial.
Preventive maintenance	Maintaining scheduled upkeep and improvement to equipment so equipment can actually improve with age is called the preventive maintenance.
Trade show	A type of exhibition or forum where manufacturers can display their products to current as well as prospective buyers is referred to as trade show.
Advertising	Advertising refers to paid, nonpersonal communication through various media by organizations and individuals who are in some way identified in the advertising message.
Public relations	Public relations refers to the management function that evaluates public attitudes, changes policies and procedures in response to the public's requests, and executes a program of action and information to earn public understanding and acceptance.
Sales management	Planning the selling program and implementing and controlling the personal selling effort of the firm is called sales management.

Chapter 17. Managing Within Your Company

Chapter 17. Managing Within Your Company

Hierarchy	A system of grouping people in an organization according to rank from the top down in which all subordinate managers must report to one person is called a hierarchy.
Competition	In business, competition occurs when rival organizations with similar products and services attempt to gain customers.
Budget	A financial plan that sets forth management's expectations for revenues and, based on those expectations, allocates the use of specific resources throughout the firm is called budget.
Expense	An expense refers to costs involved in operating a business, such as rent, utilities, and salaries.
Controlling	A management function that involves determining whether or not an organization is progressing toward its goals and objectives, and taking corrective action if it is not is called controlling.
Revenue	Revenue refers to the total amount of money a business earns in a given period by selling goods and services. The value of what is received for goods sold, services rendered.
Sales forecast	Sales forecast refers to the maximum total sales of a product that a firm expects to sell during a specified time period under specified environmental conditions and its own marketing efforts.
Gross margin	How much a firm earned by buying and selling merchandise is a gross margin. It is an ambiguous phrase that expresses the relationship between gross profit and sales revenue.
Margin	A deposit by a buyer in stocks with a seller or a stockbroker, as security to cover fluctuations in the market in reference to stocks that the buyer has purchased but for which he has not paid is a margin. Commodities are also traded on margin.
Evaluation	The consumer's appraisal of the product or brand on important attributes is called evaluation.
Loyalty	Marketers tend to define customer loyalty as making repeat purchases. Some argue that it should be defined attitudinally as a strongly positive feeling about the brand.
Interest	Interest refers to the payment the issuer of the bond makes to the bondholders for use of the borrowed money. It is the return to capital achieved over time or as the result of an event.
Marketing mix	The marketing mix approach to marketing is a model of crafting and implementing marketing strategies. It stresses the "mixing" or blending of various factors in such a way that both organizational and consumer (target markets) objectives are attained.
Cash flow	In finance, cash flow refers to the amounts of cash being received and spent by a business during a defined period of time, sometimes tied to a specific project. Most of the time they are being used to determine gaps in the liquid position of a company.
Complexity	The technical sophistication of the product and hence the amount of understanding required to use it is referred to as complexity. It is the opposite of simplicity.
Tangible	Having a physical existence is referred to as the tangible. Personal property other than real estate, such as cars, boats, stocks, or other assets.
Content	Content refers to all digital information included on a website, including the presentation form-text, video, audio, and graphics.
Options	Options give the owner the right but not the obligation to buy or sell an underlying security at a set price for a given time period.
Corporate policy	Dimension of social responsibility that refers to the position a firm takes on social and political issues is referred to as corporate policy.

Chapter 17. Managing Within Your Company

Chapter 17. Managing Within Your Company

Performance measurement	The process by which someone evaluates an employee's work behaviors by measurement and comparison with previously established standards, documents the results, and communicates the results to the employee is called performance measurement.
Corporate culture	The whole collection of beliefs, values, and behaviors of a firm that send messages to those within and outside the company about how business is done is the corporate culture.
Organizational culture	Widely shared values within an organization that provide coherence and cooperation to achieve common goals are referred to as a organizational culture.
Automation	Automation allows machines to do work previously accomplished by people.
Account executive	The individual who serves as the liaison between the advertising agency and the client is the account executive. The account executive is responsible for managing all of the services the agency provides to the client and representing the agency's point of view to the client.
Distribution	Distribution is one of the four aspects of marketing. A distribution business is the middleman between the manufacturer and retailer or (usually)in commercial or industrial the business customer.
Participation	Participation refers to the process of giving employees a voice in making decisions about their own work.
Insurance	A means for persons and businesses to protect themselves against the risk of loss is insurance.
Outbound	Communications originating inside an organization and destined for customers, prospects, or other people outside the organization are called outbound.
Team selling	Using an entire team of professionals in selling to and servicing major customers is referred to as team selling.
Product line	A group of products that are physically similar or are intended for a similar market are called the product line.
Extension	Extension refers to an out-of-court settlement in which creditors agree to allow the firm more time to meet its financial obligations. A new repayment schedule will be developed, subject to the acceptance of creditors.
Purchasing	Purchasing refers to the function in a firm that searches for quality material resources, finds the best suppliers, and negotiates the best price for goods and services.
Advertising campaign	A comprehensive advertising plan that consists of a series of messages in a variety of media that center on a single theme or idea is referred to as an advertising campaign.
Financial control	A process in which a firm periodically compares its actual revenues, costs, and expenses with its projected ones is called financial control.

Go to **Cram101.com** for the Practice Tests for this Chapter.

Chapter 17. Managing Within Your Company

Chapter 18. Managing Your Career

Marketing	The American Marketing Association suggests that Marketing is "the process of planning and executing the pricing, promotion, and distribution of goods, ideas, and services to create exchanges that satisfy individual and organizational goals."
Management	Management characterizes the process of leading and directing all or part of an organization, often a business, through the deployment and manipulation of resources. Early twentieth-century management writer Mary Parker Follett defined management as "the art of getting things done through people."
International Business	International business refers to any firm that engages in international trade or investment.
Exchange	The trade of things of value between buyer and seller so that each is better off after the trade is called the exchange.
Exhibit	Exhibit refers to a copy of a written instrument on which a pleading is founded, annexed to the pleading and by reference made a part of it. Any paper or thing offered in evidence and marked for identification.
Incentive	A reward offered by a marketer to a prospective customer in return for furnishing information or making a purchase is referred to as an incentive.
Compensation	A payment that is given or recieved as reparation for a service or loss is referred to as compensation.
Capital	Contributions of money and other property to a business made by the owners of the business are capital.
Interest	Interest refers to the payment the issuer of the bond makes to the bondholders for use of the borrowed money. It is the return to capital achieved over time or as the result of an event.
Inventory	Inventory refers to physical material purchased from suppliers, which may or may not be reworked for sale to customers. A unique element of services-the need for and cost of having a service provider available.
Marketing management	Marketing management refers to the process of planning and executing the conception, pricing, promotion, and distribution of ideas, goods, and services to create mutually beneficial exchanges.
Appeal	Appeal refers to the act of asking an appellate court to overturn a decision after the trial court's final judgment has been entered.
Industry	Industry refers to a group of firms offering products that are close substitutes for each other.
Missionary sales	A type of sales where the emphasis is on performing supportive activities and services rather than generating or taking orders is called missionary sales.
Promotion	Promotion refers to all the techniques sellers use to motivate people to buy products or services. An attempt by marketers to inform people about products and to persuade them to participate in an exchange.
Policy	Similar to a script in that a policy can be a less than completely rational decision-making method. Involves the use of a pre-existing set of decision steps for any problem that presents itself.
Communication	Communication refers to the social process in which two or more parties exchange information and share meaning.
Insurance	A means for persons and businesses to protect themselves against the risk of loss is insurance.

Go to **Cram101.com** for the Practice Tests for this Chapter.

Chapter 18. Managing Your Career

Chapter 18. Managing Your Career

Applicant	In many tribunal and administrative law suits, the person who initiates the claim is called the applicant.
Assessment	Collecting information and providing feedback to employees about their behavior, communication style, or skills is an assessment.
Manager	A person who is formally responsible for supporting the work efforts of other people is a manager.
Aptitude	An aptitude is an innate inborn ability to do a certain kind of work. Aptitudes may be physical or mental. Many of them have been identified and are testable.
Broker	An agent who bargains or carries on negotiations in behalf of the principal as an intermediary between the latter and third persons in transacting business relative to the acquisition of contractual rights, or to the sale or purchase of property the custody of which is not entrusted to him or her for the purpose of discharging the agency is called a broker.
Stockbroker	A registered representative who works as a market intermediary to buy and sell securities for clients is a stockbroker.
Evaluation	The consumer's appraisal of the product or brand on important attributes is called evaluation.
Marketing Plan	Marketing plan refers to a road map for the marketing activities of an organization for a specified future period of time, such as one year or five years.
Mistake	In contract law a mistake is incorrect understanding by one or more parties to a contract and may be used as grounds to invalidate the agreement. Common law has identified three different types of mistake in contract: unilateral mistake, mutual mistake, and common mistake.
Customer service	The ability of logistics management to satisfy users in terms of time, dependability, communication, and convenience is called the customer service.
Content	Content refers to all digital information included on a website, including the presentation form-text, video, audio, and graphics.
Independent contractor	A person who contracts with a principal to perform some task according to his own methods, and who is not under the principal's control regarding the physical details of the work. Under the Restatement of Agency, an independent contractor may or may not be an agent.
Product	Any physical good, service, or idea that satisfies a want or need is called product. Product in project management is a physical entity created as a result of project work.
Economy	The income, expenditures, and resources that affect the cost of running a business and household are called an economy.
Honor	Payment of a drawer's properly drawn check by the drawee bank is referred to as honor.
Corporation	A form of business organization that is owned by owners, called shareholders, who have no inherent right to manage the business, and is managed by a board of directors that is elected by the shareholders is called a corporation.
Competition	In business, competition occurs when rival organizations with similar products and services attempt to gain customers.
Preparation	Preparation refers to usually the first stage in the creative process. It includes education and formal training.
Personnel	A collective term for all of the employees of an organization. Personnel is also commonly used to refer to the personnel management function or the organizational unit responsible for administering personnel programs.

Go to **Cram101.com** for the Practice Tests for this Chapter.

Chapter 18. Managing Your Career

Chapter 18. Managing Your Career

Consideration	Consideration in contract law, a basic requirement for an enforceable agreement under traditional contract principles, defined in this text as legal value, bargained for and given in exchange for an act or promise. In corporation law, cash or property contributed to a corporation in exchange for shares, or a promise to contribute such cash or property.
Buyer	A buyer refers to a role in the buying center with formal authority and responsibility to select the supplier and negotiate the terms of the contract.
Strategic plan	The formal document that presents the ways and means by which a strategic goal will be achieved is a strategic plan. A long-term flexible plan that does not regulate activities but rather outlines the means to achieve certain results, and provides the means to alter the course of action should the desired ends change.
Management development	The process of training and educating employees to become good managers and then monitoring the progress of their managerial skills over time is management development.
Career management	The process of implementing organizational career planning is called career management.
Credibility	The extent to which a source is perceived as having knowledge, skill, or experience relevant to a communication topic and can be trusted to give an unbiased opinion or present objective information on the issue is called credibility.
Puffery	Advertising or other sales presentations that praise the item to be sold using subjective opinions, superlatives, or exaggerations, vaguely and generally, stating no specific facts is called puffery.
Partnership	In the common law, a partnership is a type of business structure in which partners share with each other the profits or losses of the business undertaking in which they have all invested.
Options	Options give the owner the right but not the obligation to buy or sell an underlying security at a set price for a given time period.
Learning organization	A firm, which values continuous learning and is consistently looking to adapt and change with its environment is referred to as learning organization.
Sales management	Planning the selling program and implementing and controlling the personal selling effort of the firm is called sales management.
Holding	The holding is a court's determination of a matter of law based on the issue presented in the particular case. In other words: under this law, with these facts, this result.
Mentoring	Mentoring refers to a developmental relationship between a more experienced mentor and a less experienced partner referred to as a mentee or protégé. Usually - but not necessarily - the mentor/protégé pair will be of the same sex.
Mentor	An experienced employee who supervises, coaches, and guides lower-level employees by introducing them to the right people and generally being their organizational sponsor is a mentor.
Closing	The finalization of a real estate sales transaction that passes title to the property from the seller to the buyer is referred to as a closing. Closing is a sales term which refers to the process of making a sale. It refers to reaching the final step, which may be an exchange of money or acquiring a signature.
Marketing research	Marketing research refers to the analysis of markets to determine opportunities and challenges, and to find the information needed to make good decisions.

Go to **Cram101.com** for the Practice Tests for this Chapter.